GEEK DEEP

TAPPING THE LIMITLESS POTENTIAL OF
MASTERS, MAKERS, AND MISSIONARIES
ON THE FRINGE

MATTHEW MEULENERS
ALEXIS LAVERDIERE & NATHALIE RAHNER

PUBLISHED BY:

FOCUS
SPEAKING CONSULTING TRAINING

*Robin,
I'm so appreciative of our partnership! Hope you enjoy the book.*

Printed in the United States of America

First Printing, 2019

ISBN 978-0-578-58109-5

FOCUS Training, Inc.
531 S. Water Street
Milwaukee, WI 53204

www.focustraining.com

Illustrations by Nicholas Mork and Erica Vanden Busch

To my co-authors Nat and Alexis, thank you so much.

I talked about writing this book for over seven years. Once I actually started, it took two more years of writing and research to get a draft on paper. Along the way I stopped often, distracted by other priorities or stuck in a creative rut. Turns out I don't geek on writing books.

There are two good reasons this finished product rests in your hands today: Alexis Laverdiere and Nathalie Rahner. They did research, gave feedback, wrote proposals, edited copy, and contacted, scheduled, and met with dozens of geeks. More than that, they kept this project alive over the course of many months when I might have left it to die on a shelf. Geek Deep is a product of their hard work, insight, and commitment to someone else's dream.

Special thanks also to...

Nick Mork for design work that captured the perfect vibe for our project and Erica Vanden Busch for illustrations that make some pretty geeky concepts come to life on the page.

My patient wife Carolyn who knows that real inspiration involves gentle prodding and encouragement, sometimes for years.

CONTENTS

WHAT IS A GEEK?   1

GEEK DEEP   5
CENTER OF GRAVITY   12
MASTERS, MAKERS, AND MISSIONARIES   13

INTRODUCTION   17
USE THE FORCE   26

MASTERS   29
MEET A GEEK #1   30
GEEKS DON'T QUIT   35
MASTERS OF THE UNIVERSE   38
GLOSSOPHOBIA   43
GRITTY GEEKS   45
USE THE FORCE   47
MEET A GEEK #2   54

MAKERS   61
MEET A GEEK #3   62
THE COG IS THE MOTHER OF INVENTION   67
INNOVATIVE GEEKS   70
GEEKS IN SHINING ARMOR   75
USE THE FORCE   77
MEET A GEEK #4   84

MISSIONARIES 91

MEET A GEEK #5   92
MY NEAR DEATH EXPERIENCE   96
GEEK COMMUNITY BUILDERS   102
T-SHIRT MEMBERS   104
TRELLIS GEEKS   107
GEEKY INFLUENCERS   110
USE THE FORCE   114
MEET A GEEK #6   123

CONCLUSION 129

MEET A GEEK #7   130
GEEK DEEP   136
CLOSET GEEKS   141
SEARCH FOR CENTER   143

GEEK GLOSSARY 151

MEET THE GEEK 167

REFERENCES 169

WHAT
IS A GEEK?

"I believe a geek possesses certain qualities. Geeks show resilience, especially when there are hurdles. They're going to get shit done. They also demonstrate patience by being okay with the long haul and enjoying the journey. Of course they have passion, or burning desire, to care deeply. And lastly, they have bravery, meaning they're okay with wearing geekiness on their sleeves, proud to share and genuinely excited about what they're doing. A geek won't let anything stop them from sharing that joy with others."

Alex, Creative Director at Airbnb

"I think I have a better sense of personal style than a lot of geeks in my industry do! The visual effects uniform tends to be a T-shirt from the last movie you worked on, shorts, and flip flops.

My definition of "geek" is someone who is unendingly enthusiastic and passionate about something, maybe bordering on obsession. A key point is they don't care what other people think about their passion and maintain their individuality, even when unpopular."

Kathy, Lighting Designer & Visual Effects Artist

"I was raised to believe that being a nerd is cool and being a geek is not cool. Then, I realized that language is not really effective at doing anything. I think that what it means to be a geek is that we are here just loving something, giving more than anyone else would. Parents are often geeks for their children, you know? They put everything they have into raising them, knowing more about their children than anyone else in the world.
To me, that is the geekdom in a sense; having an obsessive passion for something versus just being someone that plays on their computer all the time. You can add adjectives and nouns to specify what type of geek, but the concept is still the same. To me, a geek just means that you are better than other people in a specific area and you put in the time to be able to do that."

Conrad, 2014 North American Scrabble Champion

"I heard a definition once and I am not sure that I agree with it; A nerd is a person who knows all the details and a geek is the person that dresses up. Geek and nerds are very interchangeable these days. I prefer being called a geek, although I don't really think that it matters. Everyone geeks out on something! If you aren't geeking out, you are missing out!"

Sam, Film Industry Artist, Craftsperson, Fighter and
2013 International Jousting Tournament Long Sword Champion

"I think that geeks are passionate people who are not trying to impress anyone. They are not afraid to really get into something and learn about it."

Dylan, Entrepreneur & Co-Founder of Crowdcast and DailyPage

"I would define a geek as someone who is intellectually obsessive, who departs from the physicality of something and narrows in on a particular focus, who spends time in other worlds. Geeks always find their tribes later on in life. In high school, the athletic people can find their tribes in the sports they play, but geeks sometimes have to wait until they are in their 30s [to find their tribe], and that is fine; it is not a race.

Geeks were always the sidekick to the hero, now geeks are the heroes."

Kim, Artist & Scientist

"Being a geek has traditionally been used in a derogatory way for people who are into "nerdy" interests, such as sci-fi, computers, etc. I think in this day and age though, the meaning has altered to mean anybody who is passionate about their interests."

Karen, Youtuber & Graphic Designer

"I think everybody's geek changes, depending on what stage they are at in their life. Whatever makes you happy."

Lynn, Founder of Oak & Shield Pub

GEEK
DEEP

I can very clearly remember when it all started. I was about eight years old when I realized I was a geek. My family and I were visiting my aunt and uncle's place one summer weekend, and while the adults lounged around the living room, we kids were sitting in the basement trying to stay cool.

Suddenly, my uncle appeared at the bottom of the stairs, a serious look on his face. He took the TV remote from us, reached into the entertainment center for a VHS tape, and announced with some gravity that it was time...

Uncle Scott pushed play on his VCR. As a line of yellow text climbed the screen over a field of stars, I heard, for the first time, John Williams' score blasting out of the hi-fi, wood-paneled speakers.

In that moment a shiver ran through my spine, as if a piece of my DNA had just aligned itself to its true place in the world. I was swept, body and mind, into a galaxy far far away. I walked away that day a new person. That was only *A New Hope*, do not even ask how I reacted to *The Empire Strikes Back*.

My *Star Wars* fascination only accelerated and my own geekiness only spread in the coming years. I would soon discover world after fantastic world in which to immerse myself.

Gene Roddenberry's aspirational stories of mankind boldly venturing forth into undiscovered country stirred hopes for my own future. J. R. R. Tolkien made me believe that with determination, sacrifice, and a little magic, even the smallest among us could overcome the most intimidating of challenges. I would go on to read *The Hobbit* more than 20 times and record my own audio book version just for the sheer fun of it.

I spent Mountain Dew-fueled nights in my cousin's basement, advancing the career of my Chaotic Good Half-Elven Ranger in our weekly *Dungeons & Dragons (D&D)* games. I always wanted to be the Dungeon Master, but never had the patience. *D&D* was my gateway to fantasy games and it eventually led to my collection of *Magic the Gathering* cards. I amassed binders full of plastic sleeve protectors and participated in local tournaments to test my killer decks.

It is a slippery slope when you unleash the geek. As a young man, I poured hundreds of hours into these worlds to develop an encyclopedic knowledge of the canon and trivia. In the process, I formed strong communities of friends who shared my passions. I thought I knew what a geek was, but it turns out that, like a brash young Rebel pilot on Dagobah, much to learn had I.

In the summer of 1997 I discovered my cousin was working on a geeky project that went beyond anything we had ever attempted before. Chris had always been the superior geek, the Yoda to my Luke. He was the first to suggest we all wear costumes to the *Renaissance Festival*, first to write his own role-playing adventure instead of just buying a pre-written set, first to sign us up for a gaming tournament in the back room of the hobby store, and suddenly... *the next level of geekiness*.

When I walked into Chris's basement I noticed the pool table was strewn with a strange assortment of materials and tools. Pliers and tin snips rested among what looked to be every

Tupperware container my aunt owned, all overflowing with small shiny metal rings. Two massive spools of steel wire and an odd mechanical contraption, which looked a bit like a rotisserie, sat prominently in the center of the table.

Wearing heavy leather work gloves and leaning over the table, Chris looked deep in concentration on this mysterious task.

"Uhhhhhhh?" I inquired articulately.

Chris kept his head down, focused on the process of meticulously wrapping the heavy wire around a steel rod. He finally replied, "I'm making chain mail." Obviously.

For the uninitiated, chain mail was a form of armor used largely for protection in medieval combat. Today this armor is more commonly used when training attack dogs or swimming with small sharks. Chain mail was a critical form of protective wear for soldiers, lawmen, and brigands from the early third century up until as recently as World War I, though it was decidedly outdated at that point.

Comprised of many small rings of linked metal forming a mesh material, chain mail offers excellent flexibility and effective protection against slashing attacks from bladed weapons such as swords or daggers. While the suit offers only relatively weak protection against the sort of blunt-force trauma caused by a mace or war hammer, a coat of mail, also called a hauberk, can be paired with a padded undercoat to mitigate this concern. It would be, without question, on my list of required supplies in a *zombie apocalypse survival kit*.

Chris took on this project in the pre-Google dark ages, so he rather impressively worked through the process with nothing beyond a little advice from friends and *lots* of trial and error.

Fifteen years later, in research for my TEDx talk, I spent roughly 90 seconds online searching "Make Your Own Chain mail," and discovered detailed sets of instructions, dozens of walk through videos, and even specialized tools for sale.

Making chain mail is an incredible process! I remember being truly impressed by my cousin's passion and drive. I also remember telling few friends about it and not really being surprised when their reactions were those of confused scorn. In high school, the guy who makes his own chain mail armor is rarely found at the top of the social food chain.

We were geeks. The label was a difficult one to wear at times, and by that I mean all of grades 6-12. I managed to maintain a small group of friends with similar interests, but suffice it to say I was not going to the A-list parties or sitting at the cool table at lunch. I held back from putting my genuine self out there, working hard to fit in or stay out of sight.

My self-confidence improved during college, where I had a bit of an epiphany. The sudden transition from a high school mentality (a need to fit in) shifted into a focused effort to stand out. At Madison, in a sea of 40,000 undergrads, I found myself wanting to be seen as a unique and interesting individual rather than blend into the crowd.

This new motivation was what finally enabled me to lay claim to my geekiness. I did what Chris was somehow brave enough to do so many years earlier; *I let my geek flag fly*. I openly told people I watched *Dragon Ball Z* and had taken one of my senior pictures in a *Starfleet* uniform. I pulled out my *Magic* cards in the residence hall lounge and challenged people to a match. I organized a field trip to the Renn Faire. The change was emotionally freeing and unlocked a hidden potential in me, which eventually led to my current line of thinking, our team's research, and this book about geeks.

Let us first address the word geek. The term can feel like a pejorative implying someone is peculiar, but I identify a geek as someone who is fully immersed in what they love.

Geeks obsess. Even in the face of social norms calling for moderation, they cannot help but love what they love. Frequently, this obsession places them on the fringes of society. When I talk about geeks I am describing those with a character trait I deeply admire and to which I aspire.

I have been a professional leadership trainer for 20 years. My job has given me the opportunity to teach in classrooms and convention centers for all kinds of audiences. In my talks, I have found myself in the habit of confessing to groups of leaders about my love of all things science fiction and fantasy in connection with lessons about trust, vulnerability, or relationship building.

One day as I was preparing to speak with a large group of college students, I decided to do something a little crazy. I wore a *Star Trek* uniform under my business suit. Yes, I own a Star Fleet captain's uniform shirt (the same since high school). As I reached the part in my presentation where I share my many geeky secrets, I unbuttoned my shirtfront like the Man of Steel to reveal my uniform underneath.

The response was powerful, and has been every time since. The shocked looks from the audience members as I present my surprise striptease typically evolves into nervous laughter, then recognition, as the crowd begins to processes my symbolic gesture.

Whether I'm speaking to corporate leaders or college students, the response has been consistent. The willingness of someone on stage in front of hundreds of strangers to cast aside all pretense of being cool starts as a shock, and quickly turns into a wave of support. I came to believe that my audience's response revealed an important truth: We all crave bold transparency. We all, in some way, wish the world could see our genuine self, proud and unafraid.

After each talk where I confess my geek tendencies, a line of geeks come out of the woodwork to chat with me. These geeks cannot wait to tell me about their own obsession and the impact it has had on their lives. Those stories acted as a catalyst for this book. Each story helped me realize I wanted to meet more geeks and learn about their lives, their communities, and their cultures.

I am still exploring what I like to call the Geekosystem, the literally thousands of sub-cultures across the world made up of dedicated enthusiasts loving something you did not know existed or rarely thought about. Over the last three years, my team and I spent long periods of time with various communities of geeks. The diversity of the Geekosystem is vast, from Bronies to beekeepers, from competitive Rubik's Cube™ clubs to the *501st Legion*. These are deeply fascinating humans with powerful stories and I am excited to introduce many of them to you in this book.

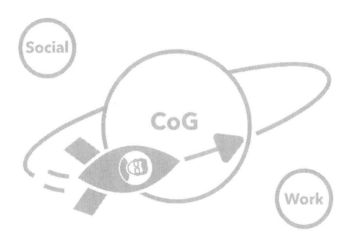

FINDING A CENTER OF GRAVITY

Communities of geeks share a common factor - a form of healthy obsession and engagement in some pursuit. To help us understand the mental state core to being a geek, I would like to offer up a metaphor: the Center of Gravity (CoG). In physics, the center of gravity can be thought of as the point at which the full weight of an object is concentrated. If you imagine a planet, the center is the point at the core around which everything is being pulled. For geeks, we can think of the metaphorical

Center of Gravity (CoG) as an irresistible focus of interest and attention. The geek is powerfully drawn to their CoG and this pull generates motion in much the same way that gravity pulls an object to the ground.

The Center of Gravity's powerful drive manifests truly valuable behaviors and can be tied to recognized success in the fields of business, education, and beyond. The very traits that make geeks appear strange to the mainstream are the same that make them great.

Geeks persist through failure, rejection, and the monotonous grind that often accompanies real progress. Even though some geeks do wear capes, they are not superhuman. Geeks are ordinary people embracing their Center of Gravity and allowing their passions to drive them.

In this book I argue that obsessive oddballs are tapping into a potential we all share. Using a diverse array of geeks and their communities as examples, I will offer up some suggestions for unlocking geeky energy to accomplish more, and grow as a professional and as a leader.

MASTERS, MAKERS, AND MISSIONARIES

Like a meteorite glowing with gamma radiation, the Center of Gravity manifests powerful traits in geeks. These *powers* allow geeks to become Masters, Makers, and Missionaries.

This premise is the core argument of this book: Geeking out on something unlocks a great potential for success. Each of these three characteristics will be broken down at length as you continue reading.

- Part 1 will introduce you to **Masters,** the savvy geeks who have developed complex skills from hours of continuous grit and determination.

- Part 2 will reveal **Makers,** the innovative geeks who complete epic and innovative projects others just cannot.

- Part 3 will explore **Missionaries,** the visionary geeks who transform the world with shared knowledge and community-building behaviors.

If you are a self-identified geek, I hope reading this book can be a journey of reflection and growth for you. If you are not, challenge yourself to make this an opportunity for discovery.

UNLOCKING HIDDEN POTENTIAL

This book was not just written for those with Darth Vader tattoos or a master-level Scrabble rank. I certainly hope geeks enjoy it, but my intention in writing this book is to explain the Geekosystem to those unfamiliar with it. I want to point out that the people living on the fringe of society have managed to do what most of us have been working our whole lives to: *unlock our potential*.

Human beings learn in many ways, one of the most powerful being by example. Our learning is strongly influenced by observing model humans who are able to do the things we want. As we gathered research for this book, we met a great number of people and organizations modeling geek traits in useful ways. We observed many of the same keys to success that business gurus and self-help books tell us we can only achieve with a particular system or training. Around the world geeks are achieving success all on their own *and you can too*.

New professionals, you are striving to master new skills and discover what moves you. You have been sold the new American Dream to follow your passion and do what you love for a living. The problem? Nobody has given you a road map to achieve this dream. You are cultivating a skill set and working hard to make your mark on the world. Perhaps you are wondering, "How can I stay energized and patient through the difficult process of building my career?" Geeks are modeling the passion and grit that you need.

Entrepreneurs, you want to change the world or at least introduce to it something new and exciting. Do you want to inspire backers to believe in you and support you on your mission? You should know geeks are instinctively creating cult followings and bold innovations as you read this very page.

Business leaders, you want to grow a community of customers, build a strong organization, and spread powerful brand messages. You need to understand how to nurture and work alongside talent that pushes further than the mainstream. Geeks can fuel the transformation you are looking for.

As a trainer, I care less that you remember *what* I say in this book than I do that you *act on it*. At several points in the book you will find a section called **Use the Force**, in which I will offer some suggestions on how to directly apply key ideas in your own life as a leader. These tactical suggestions and questions for reflection are focused on the work environment, but often apply just as well to the rest of your life.

Along the way, I make a *lot* of geek culture references to illustrate the ideas I am discussing. Frankly, I cannot help myself. If you geek like I do, you will understand what I mean when I drop a line like, "I thought they smelled bad on the outside."

If you are not as geeky and are ever feeling lost by these references, fear not! Whenever possible, these little shout-outs to geek culture will appear in italics and be listed alphabetically in the **Geek Glossary**. Flip back to find a concise summary of the movie, show, comic, or whatever I was rambling about.

HEARTFELT THANKS

I want to take a moment to recognize the amazing openness and vulnerability of the geeks we interviewed. It takes an act of bravery to talk to a stranger in depth about your deeply held passions, particularly if society views them as odd.

Thank you to all whose stories are featured in these pages or in our blog posts, and to the hundreds of others who answered surveys, stopped to chat at conventions, or welcomed us into your hobby shops, hotel ballrooms, comic book stores, basements, and parents' kitchens. *We geek on you.*

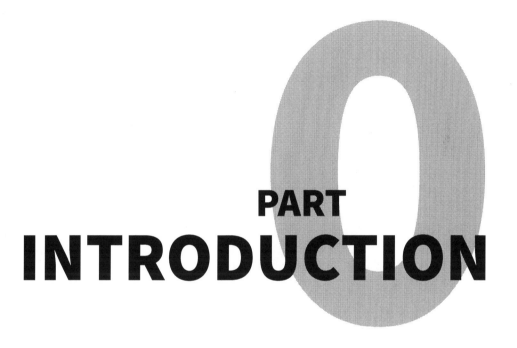

PART
INTRODUCTION

SWIMMING UPSTREAM

Restrictive norms are pervasive in our society. Think about it: People who show up for a movie on opening night are accepted as fanatics, but those who show up in costumes? *Weirdos.* We put those folks on the evening news to show everyone just how wacky they are.

Tell your coworkers you are fascinated by the Civil War and they will nod politely. Show them the photos of you in your navy blue officer's frock from your recent reenactment weekend and you become the subject of lunchroom gossip.

For most of my life I have been hearing the same inspiring message repackaged by various leaders: "Follow your passion," "Do what you love and you will never have to work a day in your life," and "Live your dreams."

I heard this from Roosevelt, Jobs, Mandela, Gaiman, my parents, my teachers, my high school guidance counselor, the student speaker at every graduation I have ever attended, and the older gentleman I sat next to on a bus from Minneapolis to Madison as a college student. They all told me some version of this same idealized model for living one's best life. If you want to be happy and make an impact on the world, embrace what you love and pay no mind to the haters.

This mantra is echoed in posters, self-help books, movies, and training programs. Young people hear this message and visualize a future where they are accepted and engaged in a life of purpose and passion. It seems as if all one would have to do to be successful is discover a Center of Gravity and go after it.

Running counter to this concept, however, is the fact that human nature includes a powerful need to fit in with a group.

Starting in elementary and middle school, the desire to be accepted drives kids to build social norms and then fall in line. I can clearly remember the anxiety I had about not owning the right brand of jeans or whether my collection of Pogs™ was cool enough to make the right impression. These practices are reinforced over and over as young people grow up and shape their identity and world-view.

The mainstream establishes a safe zone of acceptable behaviors, interests, and pursuits. Those who wander beyond this zone risk being ostracized and isolated, while those who conform are rewarded and protected.

The mainstream is fueled by a very old fear. As humans, we are hardwired to be cautious of the unknown. Being afraid served humans well long ago, preventing our curious ancestors from eating the wrong berries or waltzing into a mysterious dark cave. In balance with our powerful curiosity and creativity, a healthy aversion to the risky unknown helped keep our ancestors alive long enough to ensure our existence today. When placed in a modern context, however, the instinct to fear what we do not recognize or understand can become a major hindrance.

This fear lives in our amygdala, a part of the brain that developed so long ago that we often refer to it as a part of our "reptilian" brain. The center of survival, this region controls critical impulses like hunger and fear. It is powerful, yet simple.

Because of its critical role the amygdala often has priority over other brain functions. Most importantly, it has the ability to overpower the frontal cortex, the part of our brain that provides executive functions like critical thinking, empathy, strategy, creativity, and complex learning.

Our amygdala offers three basic options for confronting fear, none of which translate very well into polite society:

1.) Fight

We lash out at what we fear, namely the things we do not understand. The unknown may be a shark, or a person who geeks out on things we don't understand. Fear leads to slander, bullying, or even violence. The fight response encompasses all sorts of attacks on geeks and geek culture, from verbal abuse in the high school lunchroom to the incredible Satanic Panic targeting *Dungeons & Dragons* in the 1970s.

2.) Flight

We retreat from what we fear or hold it at a distance. When our amygdala chooses the flight response to social fears we ostracize geeks, even choosing to back away from existing relationships when we discover the person is into weird stuff. Retreat most strongly reinforces the idea of the fringe vs. the mainstream, as it isolates geeks from the rest of society.

3.) Freeze

We offer no reaction to what we fear, hoping that if we pretend it does not exist then it might simply go away. We repeat little mantras like, "I'm just not into any of that sci-fi robots and wizards stuff" without ever taking the time to learn more than the minimum surface impressions. While this response is not as harmful to the geeks themselves, it can be most dangerous to one's own ability to discover a CoG for themselves and leverage all the benefits of geek life we are exploring in this book.

The most challenging thing about controlling these responses is that they are mostly involuntary. Our behaviors are hard-wired into our brains and reinforced throughout our lives by role models, social hierarchies, and news media. You are unlikely to find much success in attempting to reprogram the ancient amygdala, so what *can* you do to fight the fear response?

I believe the answer lies up front in the cortex. Fight, flight, or freeze responses are triggered by fear and uncertainty. The reptilian brain does not pause to ask whether our fear is based in fact, rumor, or wild speculation, it simply reacts in order to protect. The frontal cortex, on the other hand, loves to ask questions, gather data, and analyze arguments. Once it pauses to complete these actions, the frontal cortex squashes the ambiguity driving our fear and it disappears like a Dementor to a Patronus charm.

As an individual, you can control your own interactions with the geeks around you. In groups, organizations, and communities, we lose some of this control. Let yourself feel the fear, but train yourself to follow up on your reaction and question it.

Start by asking some questions about what sounds so foreign and strange. Geeks will be thrilled to tell you more if you are willing to take a chance and ask. The more data you gather the less unknown a concept becomes and the less influence your amygdala has over your thought processes and reactions.

"Why did I feel uncomfortable at the dinner party when Mitch from work showed me his massive Disney memorabilia collection? Normally, I am not rude to people like that, so what drove my reaction this time? Are these reactions coming from a place of fear? What lives at the root of that fear, and what happens if I dig a little deeper?"

The power of the mainstream is pervasive and can be difficult to shift. These thoughts and norms are not necessarily a problem, but when we participate in forcing them on others we become complicit in a bigger problem.

Across the modern world we are sending a painfully mixed message to students, employees, and citizens: Following your dreams is the path to success, and doing what you love matters, but stay within the lines if you want to be accepted and supported.

Well, which is it?

To find our answer, we must redefine the mainstream through our own actions and reactions, through the way we build communities and organizations, and most critically, through how we pursue our own passions. In our teams, our families, our circles, and eventually the larger community, we can craft a set of mainstream norms where the central shared value is discovering and embracing your Center of Gravity.

Instead of a short list of approved interests, let us work on making *interest itself* the common ground that validates our inclusion in society. It is possible to make the shift; I have seen it happen organically in subcultures across the Geekosystem. Pockets of geeks are modeling the first bold step, the simple choice key to unlocking our greater potential: Making our deep passions public. Or, as I call it, letting your geek flag fly.

Geeks come out and say it. They rock the shirt, cape, armor, or costume. They tell their friends, post, or invite us to check it out. I am not referring to the geeks-in-secret, hiding their guilty pleasure from the world. The CoG is part of the proud public identity of a Supergeek, not a Clark Kent.

You might be thinking to yourself, "Sci-fi is cool now. This is a lot easier than you are making it out to be. Geeks are not the outcasts they once were."

I understand this argument, but must respectfully disagree. Yes, the lovable group of geeks on *The Big Bang Theory* have humanized some of these subcultures. And yes, *Star Wars* is possibly more popular than it has ever been. Even the cool middle school kids are wearing R2-D2 backpacks. However, I still get raised eyebrows when my colleagues see my shared calendar event for a *D&D* game night.

The mainstream may have shifted slightly, but it still reigns. The old targets for fear are still there, even if the newest generation has embraced some of them.

New targets now exist. Can you even begin to imagine how much shade is thrown at your average 33-year-old Bronie when he confesses his passion? Picture how your coworkers would react if they discovered that you spent 20+ hours a week managing your Reddit presence.

No, I am afraid this problem is not fixed by making individual interests cooler. The ebb and flow of trends in pop culture is zero-sum. When building robots starts to get hip, something else become uncomfortable and weird enough to take its place on our cultural fringe.

This effect is unfortunate because geeking out is actually a prerequisite mindset of top performers in many settings. An ability to commit to that which moves you without shame or timidity is powerful. Great athletes practice to the exclusion of a social life. Great artists sleep in their studios. Great business leaders obsessively work to perfect their product and processes. And, none of the great feel they need to hide their passions as if they were shameful.

The most successful among us wear their obsessions like a badge of honor. The world should stop and recognize the parallels between those we recognize as the greatest in society and those we shun as social outsiders.

As a leader at any level, you can reap the benefits of the geeks around you by reaching out to those in your company, your community, and your customer base:

- Invite geeks into the conversation or ask for their help and opinions.

- Give them your new idea and let them play with it.

- Create an environment that welcomes them.

- Give them the opportunity to be part of a community of peers who respect their passion and even fuel it.

- Then sit back and watch them create, explore, and share.

As an individual, you can personally benefit from letting your own geek flag fly. I may have buried the lead here, but the most important lesson I learned over the years of finding, observing, and interviewing geeks is this: *Geeks are happy.* **Really happy. Not indulged. Not comfy. They are deeply engaged and fulfilled by the way they are living their lives.**

Sure, they are enjoying themselves, but as we will see, it is not all fun and games when you are pursuing an obsession. Deep happiness is achieved by the fulfillment of your higher-order needs. I struggled to understand what Maslow meant by self-actualized, until I met dozens of folks in the Geekosystem who fully understood their purpose and knew why they were here.

Geeks have given themselves permission to do what they love, letting go of some of the restrictive social pressures that burden us.

Instead of building another addition to your house, or buying the same luxury car your neighbor owns, consider instead how it might feel to truly embrace your individual interests and allow yourself to explore them further. Tell people about your Center of Gravity and seek a community built on shared passion.

The hardest part of geeking your way to happiness is the first step: finding and recognizing your CoG. But once you take it there are vast communities of passionate people just waiting to share the experience with you.

Take a deep breath, reach out, and **GEEK DEEP**.

 ## USE THE FORCE

How can you utilize the CoG to better lead Geeks?

A geek's CoG is not the sole focus of his or her life. Like gravity, it is an ever-present force. The self-aware geek, or those who lead them, can leverage the Center of Gravity to amplify, drive, or redirect action.

Consider the gravity assist maneuver. This is the method by which NASA scientists use the strong gravity of a planetary body to slingshot a spacecraft to a greater speed with less fuel. With careful targeting and guidance, they use a powerful force like Jupiter's gravity well to accelerate a craft out to the edge of the solar system. The engineers targeting the spacecraft do not aim at the heart of the planet. Instead, the craft is cleverly aligned to come close enough to the planet's pull to take advantage of the force without colliding or becoming trapped in the orbit. When done right, this maneuver accelerates the craft and launches it along the desired path.

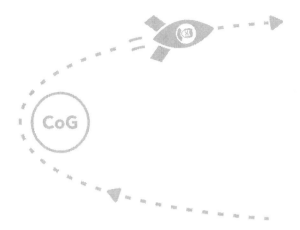

Back on Earth, the same idea can be applied to harness a geek's motivational driver, the CoG, to guide desired action. Aligning your desired behavior or outcomes closely to what a geek is passionate about can accelerate their motivation.

Let me be clear, I am not telling you to let your employees spend all their time watching Twitch streams or reading comic books in the hope it will make them more motivated. Do not directly target the center of interest. Rather, position yourself just close enough to jump-start the acceleration.

Maybe this means your software engineers earn an hour of special project coding time when they clear the customer ticket queue before Friday. Or, maybe it means leaning into the fandom craze like one of our clients did when the Brewers made the MLB playoffs. The company hosted a watch party for employees who were on target to hit their quarterly goals. Find ways to align what you need done and what people love to do and watch geeks fly!

QUESTIONS TO CONSIDER

1. Do you have a good understanding of the people you lead, their interests, and what they are geeking out on (CoG)?

2. What can you do to learn more about and engage the Centers of Gravity that exist on your team?

3. What are the behaviors you most need to change or drive in the people on your team?

4. How can you creatively align those desired behaviors to the CoGs that are common in your team? Are there ways you can give geeks permission to do what they love in a way that drives the behaviors you need?

5. Which aspects of your organization or team culture would have to shift to make this sort of interest-driven work successful? What can you do to model that culture shift as a leader?

PART

MASTERS

1

MEET A GEEK 1 - SCRABBLE CHAMPS

Scrabble is a popular board game that most Americans have played at home. Inevitably, an argument with friends about whether "ZA" is a legit play will be had (Answer: Yes, "ZA" is allowed in the official rules as a slang term for pizza). What's lesser known is the North American Scrabble championship and its geeky competitors. Scrabble was invented in the 1930s, but it was not until the 1950s when the tournament craze began and hundreds of players competed to win the title of Scrabble Champion.

In 2004, school Scrabble clubs gained popularity among student competitors. John Williams, former executive director of the National Scrabble Association (NSA), reflects on his time working with these clubs. "There was a wide range of types of kids, skill levels, and hijinks. At one tournament, we had a pair of seventh grade girls who realized their fifth-grade boy opponents were complete novices. Midway into the game, they decided to start laying random, absurd letters on the board. The boys were too intimidated to challenge and deferred on every play, so the girls won by hundreds of points. Needless to say, this particular girls' team did not win the Sportsmanship Award."

Starting out in the job, John had limited knowledge of the tournament world. "By the end of my first tournament weekend, I'd reached three critical realizations. First, there was obviously a lot more to Scrabble subculture than I'd ever realized. Secondly, there was a lot more subtlety to the tournament game than the living room version. Third, for thousands of people throughout North America, Scrabble was far more than a game. So it became my job, my mission, to recognize this curious passion and tell the story to the rest of the world."

The world of competitive Scrabble is full of fascinating personalities who rise to the top with unique approaches. Conrad was the winner of the 2014 North American Scrabble tournament. He did not care how inappropriate a word may be. If the tiles earned him the most points, he played vulgar words around family members, children, and senior citizens. To him, nothing was off limits. This cutthroat strategy is how Conrad became the youngest player ever to be crowned North American Scrabble Champion.

Conrad began playing competitive Scrabble as a teenager, building his skills by studying anagrams and the word choices of other players. "I played Scrabble with my family as a kid. In middle school and high school I was bullied. I discovered online Scrabble as an outlet to escape from school and became really good at it. People told me I should go check out a tournament. It took me a while because I was very shy. Eventually, I made it to a tournament and the adults there would tell me I was very cool; They actually gave me the time of day!"

The Scrabble community is unique. Conrad says, "It is sort of like a small town; Everyone kind of knows everyone. People will become friends will each other's friends and there are groups of people who all love each other. I have made so many close friendships throughout my [Scrabble] career, from my first love, to brothers and sisters, to family. I really saw a lot of social taboos that society would have viewed as being abnormal but that I saw as being enriching and powerful."

So, what do you need to know about the competitive world of Scrabble? If you are late, tough luck. Your clock starts without you, so being prepared is essential.

Performance-enhancing drugs are not just for physical athletes! Brain boosting supplements are taken by some before a tournament and many competitors swear they work.

Players have vast collections of dictionaries and encyclopedias they study at great length. They dedicate hundreds of hours a year building their vocabulary and practicing word recall.

The bottom line? Scrabble's biggest and best have devoted themselves completely to the game. Conrad confesses, "There may have been hobbies I could have done along the way and loved, and maybe I just chose not to do them because I was invested in the Scrabble world. You have to be obsessive in a hobby to be good at it. If not, then it's not really a hobby." Many of the top players exhibit this kind of fixation.

The 1980 World Scrabble Champion took a job as night watchman just so he would have the time to study words for hours at a time.

The 1997 World Scrabble Champion "GI Joe" Joel Sherman committed his life even more fully to the game. Although competing does not earn him a steady income, Joel acknowledges Scrabble as his career. A college dropout, Joel has never applied himself to any job as rigorously as he has to Scrabble. As the head of his own Scrabble club, Joel wakes up, plays Scrabble, goes to sleep, and repeats.

As a former champion, Conrad now sees himself as an ambassador for the game. "The way I view it, when I represent myself in public for the Scrabble community, for my friends, or for myself, I do it in order to paint Scrabble in a better light. Like many social outcasts, I have a lot of identity and self-confidence issues. As I have gotten older, I have tried to see where my place is in the world. Sometimes I question whether I can follow through with my goals. Then, I look back at Scrabble and think, 'Dude, you memorized an entire dictionary, you mastered an entire game, and became one of the top couple players in the world! Clearly, you have the ability to be good at something if you put your mind to it."

Conrad believes everyone deserves to find his or her own community of like-minded people. "I want to encourage people to find their own crowd. Whatever subculture, your life will become enriched and far more exciting than it probably was before. I look back at my life and wonder, 'What would I have done if I was not part of this subculture that allowed me to travel the world, become a champion, and make most of my dreams come true?' I want people to know that no matter what you like, there are other people out there who like that too and you should go find them."

Today, Conrad has moved on from the professional world of Scrabble. He has set his sights on a more traditional career path. After attending Carnegie Mellon University to pursue his master's degree, Conrad secured a job at Google. Although he acknowledges that he is basically retired from competitive Scrabble, Conrad confessed that it will likely always be an obsession for him. "The place the game holds in my life is too strong. Scrabble will never just be a hobby to me, it will always be an obsession. It will either be an obsession or it will be nothing. And I don't think it can be nothing. It is interwoven into my inner begin at this point."

MASTERS: GEEKS DON'T QUIT

As a kid, do you remember watching athletes and performers doing something very difficult and thinking, "I could do that." It seemed like if you just tried hard enough you could shoot a three-pointer like Jordan or juggle fire batons like the guy at the circus. Do you also remember the inevitable, crushing realization that you were wrong in your hubris? Maybe you spent most of a weekend launching yourself off the diving board at the YMCA or in your backyard trying to land a standing back flip, only to come to the sweaty conclusion it was a lot harder than it looked. You quit and went inside to watch cartoons. At least that is what I did.

Later in life these heartbreaking moments are moderated by the discovery that champion-level performers are not just mythically gifted. Instead, masters of any skill are both gifted *and* have been practicing compulsively for many long years.

LeBron James hits the gym at 5 a.m. and then drills on the court for many long hours, seven days a week. Steve Wozniak spent hundreds of hardcore nerd hours playing with computer hardware before he ever entered the spotlight as one of the co-founders of Apple. After decades of being recognized as one of the world's most renowned virtuosos, Yo Yo Ma still spends an estimated five to six hours a day practicing his cello. As many examples of this concept exist as there are high-performers, but a personal story always comes to mind for me.

Back in college, I was hanging out at a campus bar with my friend Todd, who is *very* good at foosball. By this I mean that he could easily defeat me and everyone I knew, even with a variety of significant handicaps applied. Todd would play against me one-handed, with two or three opponents, or even with a five-goal advantage. I had long since given up playing against him but would happily hop into a game on his side of the table.

On this particular Saturday night he confidently challenged a couple of guys who were occupying the only foosball table in the establishment. With some swagger in his step, Todd walked up to the table and asked to take on the winner.

I had watched this scene play out dozens of times. I knew my buddy was a shark and I looked forward to seeing the typical shocked looks of defeat and demands for a rematch. I could tell just by looking at his opponents that this match would not last very long. We would probably have rights to the table *and* a pitcher of beer in less than 10 minutes.

The actual result shattered my preconceptions. Tonight something new happened. The skinny kid who first stepped up to take on Todd's challenge crushed him. The score was not even close. Frankly, I still think the one goal Todd scored was gifted to him out of pity once the mismatch became obvious. When the dust settled on the third game, my magnanimous friend bought a round and asked his opponent the obvious question: "How in the…?"

The skinny kid proceeded to tell us that he came to this bar for several hours nearly every night just so he could play foosball. When he could not make it to the bar or spare the money to buy a cheap beer the foosball wizard practiced difficult shots and timing alone on the table in his apartment.

This mysterious foosball demigod estimated he was playing at least 50 games a week and had been on that pace for years. He was obsessed. Sometimes this enthusiast even called in late to work just so he could get in another game. Understanding the kid's crazy level of ability became easier once we realized he had invested literally thousands of his spare hours into practice and training.

The critical difference between myself and the foosball wizard lives way back in the moment a nine-year-old me gave up on trying to juggle three tennis balls in the backyard and headed inside to watch *He-Man and the Masters of the Universe*. Geeks don't. The don't quit. The obsession drives them to grind on and on until they become Masters.

MASTERS OF THE UNIVERSE

On a basic level mastery is the aggregation of vast learning. Masters have learned the knowledge and skills required to be highly capable in a specific discipline. While not every geek achieves mastery, each learns and expands his or her capabilities in pursuit of the Center of Gravity. And, I will argue, geeks are better equipped to reach mastery than the general population due to a subtle but critical natural advantage.

Mastery sounds clear, but in reality it is a bit ephemeral. It can be difficult to define because each instance of mastery is unique to a particular skill set, to the person learning, and also to the particular Master. Let me elaborate.

Mastery is...

Unique to the skill

Can you compare a virtuoso saxophone player to an ace fighter pilot, or even that same sax player to a fellow musician, like a violinist? Different skill sets have wildly divergent baselines when it comes to measuring ability, so the task of clarifying *who* constitutes a master across disciplines is a challenge.

Unique to the learner

Even if we hold skill sets constant, when comparing learners in pursuit of mastery we must consider how the potential and past experiences of each learner affects the process. For example, if you and I both attempt to learn the saxophone we would progress at different paces, struggling with different elements of the challenge.

Unique to the Master

Within a single practice area a Master will approach the craft in a way that is unique to his or her values, historical references, and preferences. In pursuit of mastery different styles emerge, which in turn define the Master's craft. Famous jazz musicians *John Coltrane* and *Charlie Parker* both undeniably mastered the saxophone but each approached his instrument and path to musical mastery in a special way.

Since mastery is hard to define with any certain clarity, let's focus our discussion on the common contributing element: *Practice*.

Masters practice, *a lot.* A disciplined, focused approach is needed to hone the skills required for challenging projects and achievements. While some areas of the Master's performance can be attributed to factors like natural ability, even a genetic miracle like Michael Phelps still practices at a monumental level to unlock his potential and transform it into a championship edge.

Yes, there are many variables skewing the baseline and making the threshold for mastery inevitably subjective, but respected thought leaders have suggested that mastering a complex skill requires between 10,000 - 25,000 hours of dedicated practice. Even if we agree to a modest 17,500 hours, this commitment is a huge undertaking.

Let's imagine you want to master the skill of customer data mining for marketing research. To log 17,500 hours of data mining practice you would need to invest four hours each day… five days a week… every week… for 17 years!

To many of us this idea is dead before it even hits the page. Would you take on this practice schedule? *Probably not.* But what if you love data mining? I mean really, deeply, cannot-stop-thinking-about-it LOVE data mining. Data is on your mind at work, on the bus, and in the shower.

What if instead of feeling like homework data mining felt like the game your parents used to forbid you to play until after your homework was completed? Or what if data mining was connected to another obsession in your life, like crunching reams of performance data to give you an edge in your fantasy baseball league?

I played the viola for a couple of years in middle school. I dreaded practice. It felt like a chore every time my parents bugged me to pull out my sheet music and grind through my assigned scales. When the orchestra program became serious enough that my lack of practice was obvious I quit immediately.

Some of my friends did not have this barrier; they even *liked* playing scales. They would look forward to getting home after school, pulling out their instrument, and losing themselves in the music for an hour. Some of those friends became extremely talented and still play today, one even professionally.

A Center of Gravity pulls the geek toward practice because it replicates or is connected to an activity that they love. Geeks would still take on the investment of time even if the payoff for all their hard work was not the mastery of a complex skill. The geek's natural advantage over the rest? They are enjoying themselves as they work.

Remember our Scrabble geeks? Matthew was the champion the year after Conrad. He explained to us that *Scrabble* is not really the game people think it is. Contrary to popular opinion, excelling at *Scrabble* is not all about having extraordinary vocabulary skills.

Players who are non-native English speakers, like those living in Southeast Asia and Africa, are some of the top competitors in the game. Many schools in Thailand actually use Scrabble to teach English to students. This means that players who cannot hold a conversation with you in English can destroy you in a game of Scrabble. They are proficient at the game because they have practice a lot.

Why do we assume winners must just have an extraordinary mastery of the English language? *Naturalness bias.*

Naturalness bias is "a hidden prejudice against those who've achieved what they have because they worked for it, and a hidden preference for those whom we think arrived at their place in life because they are naturally talented." This bias affects how we behave as leaders as well. We show preference to individuals who seem "talented" rather than investing in developing all our people.

Both *Scrabble* champions we spoke to recalled devoting hours a day studying words. They recognized they could have taken up a different hobby or done something else with their time but chose not to because they were invested.

Conrad recalls, "At the time it did not feel like a sacrifice, but when you devote yourself to just one thing, it makes it very hard to devote yourself to something else. I am the sort of person that if I care about something or someone, I am going to give my all to it, and if I don't, I am probably not going to do it at all."

This statement is a clear expression of grit. Not quitting, seeing a project through to completion, is a clear illustration of the geek as a Master.

GLOSSOPHOBIA

My first experience mastering a skill began my freshman year of high school. I admired those who could present well, and knew I wanted the confidence and skill great orators had but I was nervous and unskilled at speaking in front of large groups of people. My palms would sweat and I would lose my train of thought mid-presentation.

A lot of people can empathize with the fear of presenting. Glossophobia, the fear of public speaking, is a condition shared by more than 70 percent of the population. It took me years to become a part of the other 30 percent.

At the end of my sophomore year I ran for president of my school's chapter of DECA, a career and technical student organization focused on marketing and management. In order to run I had to complete an application, write my goals, and present a speech to our 75 members.

As I prepared for my presentation, I experienced the familiar anxiety. In response I practiced over and over again, receiving feedback and coaching from my friends, parents, and teachers. It helped. During this speech, for the first time, when I stood up in front of my peers to speak a sort of rush came over me. I still felt fearful, absolutely, but this time *I kinda liked it.*

Some people love to be scared. My wife gets a thrill from roller coasters and haunted houses. On a Halloween night she will stay up late and watch horror movies with the lights off, all alone. I do not like to be scared; I am wired differently. When my wife pulls up her latest demonic possession flick in our Netflix queue I head upstairs to crack open a comic book or my weathered copy of *The Hobbit*. The feeling of fear is not typically fun for me, except on stage.

My first big presentation felt to me the way I imagine adrenaline junkies feel as they hurl themselves out of an airplane or climb into a shark cage; I was terrified and loving it. I was hooked. I started looking for every opportunity to be in front of a crowd. As a presenter for group projects, representing our chapter at conferences, as a speaker at awards luncheons. I could not get enough. I was geeking out on public speaking and aggregating hundreds of hours practicing for the sheer joy of it.

Was it all fun along the way? A truly no-cost investment in mastery? *No*. I experienced obstacles, setbacks, and plateaus of growth through which I had to grind. Writing my first keynote speech was especially cumbersome. Months of writing and experimentation were needed just to convince myself I had created something worth sharing, not simply a 45-minute monologue packed with bad jokes.

Even the rough patches on my way to mastery were engaging in their own way, challenging my will and enticing me forward with the promise of a potential victory beyond.

I have followed my passion for presentation over the last 20 years. From my amateur days up through my career with FOCUS Training and stints as adjunct faculty, by my best estimate I have logged over 15,000 hours of direct presentation with live groups. I also spent thousands of practice hours in preparation for those opportunities. Mastery came almost without my conscious awareness, and *that* is the advantage geeks hold in acquiring new skills.

GRITTY GEEKS

Geeks have another advantage in pursuit of mastery. Love of the activity allows geeks to more easily persevere in the face of hardship, boredom, and failure. This ability to persist, often described as *grit*, is a driver of success in business, academics, *and beyond*!

Dr. Angela Duckworth, a professor at the University of Pennsylvania and MacArthur Genius grant fellow, authored the book *Grit: The Power of Passion and Perseverance*. Based on her research and classroom experiences, Duckworth argues talent is less commonly the reason for one's success. Rather, she suggests our ability to push through the difficulties we face on the path toward achievement is more heavily determined by the passion and sense of purpose we have for the activity.

Duckworth writes of Charles Darwin as an example of passion leading to success. Darwin said, "For I have always maintained that, excepting fools men did not differ much in intellect, only in zeal and hard work; and I still think this is an eminently important difference." Darwin was very intelligent, but his insights did not often come quickly. Instead his revelations required a significant amount of time to take form.

He continues, "I think I am superior to the common run of men in noticing things which easily escape attention, and in observing them carefully. My industry has been nearly as great as it could have been in observation and collection of facts. What is far more important, my love of natural science has been steadily ardent."

Darwin was described by a biographer as someone who would keep thinking about the same questions long after others would move onto different problems. His deep love of science helped him remain focused on his research throughout his entire life, turning him into one of the most recognized natural scientists in history. It sounds to me like Darwin was a huge geek.

Duckworth tested grit by measuring behavior in the sales profession. In a role where rejection is a part of daily work, after a period of six months nearly half of surveyed employees had quit their jobs. Duckworth concluded it was grit, more than any other factor, that determined who stayed and who left.

Her findings were retested in Chicago Public Schools with evaluations of which students would graduate and which students would drop out before graduation. Again, grit was the determining factor for who graduated and who dropped out, more than "how much students cared about school, how conscientious they were about their studies, and even how safe they felt at school."

The Scripps National Spelling Bee, one of the most recognizably geeky events on the planet, became a way for Duckworth to test her Grit Scale against natural aptitude. Participants had a wide range of aptitude scores. Some scored at the level of verbal prodigy and others tested at the average level for their age.

Her study found that those with higher grit measures than their peers went further in the competition. Gritty kids studied longer and competed in a greater number of spelling bees than their counterparts. Duckworth's take away from the Bee? "Our potential is one thing. What we do with it is quite another."

 ## USE THE FORCE

How can you leverage the power of a CoG to lead gritty Geeks?

If grit is an important factor in differentiating high-level performers from the rest, leaders must ask themselves how they can apply geek grit to create a more capable organization. How can businesses find potential gritty Masters and leverage their skills to create a competitive advantage?

Think about the capabilities your team is missing right now. Now think about which of those capabilities your organization will desperately need in the coming years. Which positions are most challenging for your organization to fill or keep filled?

In every organization there are various critical roles and positions requiring mastery of a specific discipline, whether that be chemical engineering, customer service, or copywriting. As a business leader, you need to discover, engage, and retain the Masters needed to fill these roles.

Let's walk through these steps together.

1.) Discovery

How does one go about finding the right people, those who geek out on the skills and abilities your business needs? Recruiting for a special set of skills may require alternative approaches to standard talent acquisition. Think about how your organization writes its job descriptions and postings. Most traditional postings focus solely on job requirements with little attention to the applicant's enthusiasm for the work. Are you advertising to applicants with a passion for the job you are offering, or simply to those who are capable of doing the job? The wording in your posting matters. If you want people who love your product that could be listed in "Requirements".

During the interview process are you asking the right sorts of questions to understand what a candidate really loves doing? Some companies incorporate passion into the process. Recruiters at Ralph Lauren ask candidates to explain what they wore to the interview and why they chose it as a way of identifying candidates who are truly passionate about fashion.

If your organization doesn't invest resources into learning how candidates spend time outside of normal work hours, consider broaching the topic. Once you uncover what gets people genuinely excited it becomes easier to identify parallels in work tasks.

If you are serious about proactively searching for the geeks your organization needs, look first to the groups and gatherings where your target geek would spend his or her time. The search is easier than you may think. If you are hunting for someone who geeks out on Client Relationship Management (CRM) tools, you would be likely to find your candidate at a CRM industry conference like Dreamforce.

Try asking your current talent where they go to geek out. You might be surprised at just how many of your talented coders can be found wandering the booths at a Comic Con or in the stands cheering on their favorite e-sports team. These sorts of events attract geeks who are looking to develop their skills, network with other fans, and celebrate their CoG in a safe space. They provide a great opportunity for you to connect.

Do not forget to look for talent in your own backyard. Customer pools are often overlooked as a source of geek talent. If you need someone who will ruthlessly beta test your product prototype, take a lesson from video game companies such as Activision.

For years, Activision, a large video game developer has been offering its biggest fans early access to upcoming games in exchange for feedback on product launches and improvements. Activision receives free labor from fans eager for a sneak-peek, releases a better end product to its target consumer, and garners huge viral marketing support from fans who tested the product and now feel a sense of pride and ownership. This is a win-win-win situation.

2.) Engagement

Truly connecting to the pre-existing pool of geeks found among your customers and employees involves showing them that they are valued and important. Create pathways that allow the voices of excited individuals to cut straight through the noise and be heard by top decision-makers or subject matter experts in the company.

Start by reading your organization's customer feedback forms and social media comments, with an open mind. So many creators, leaders, and business owners are thin-skinned and defensive of their work. This sensitivity can lead to missing out on valuable feedback and ideas in an effort to protect egos.

You can further elevate your involvement by hosting a hackathon, the latest iteration of the continuous improvement meeting. Typically, a hackathon is a one-day deep dive into area-specific process improvement. In just one gathering, cross-functional teams generate innovative approaches to organizational challenges. A deep-rooted interest in the topic or challenge to be solved is the unifying factor that brings attendees together.

One international insurance company recently implemented its own hackathon. The company placed 120 participants in 10 cross-functional teams, then asked each team to redesign how its customers process healthcare claims. In just 24 hours competing teams delivered a new model that completely reinvented the way customers monitor their health and interact with insurance providers.

The hackathon energized employees and opened the eyes of company leadership to the potential of digital technology to transform the business. The event also helped to persuade skeptical members of management that the company could deliver on a bold, high-profile customer initiative. The CEO put an end to paper processes, declaring the beginning of a zero-based company design.

The mastery you need is out there just waiting to be tapped. What are a few simple ways you can draw out and engage the geeks in and around your organization?

3.) Retention

Ironically, retaining Master talent may be the simplest challenge of all. Loyalty is at the very core of a geek's personality. They are loyal to their Center of Gravity as well as the communities they join to pursue it. As a leader, you will have to earn that loyalty. You can also leverage the "slingshot maneuver" I mentioned earlier by keeping a pipeline of engaging work flowing the Master's way.

For a more mundane task try making it more interesting by connecting it back to the employee's CoG. Immersing a geek in his or her area of interest helps the hours fly by until a project is completed.

The manager of an IT team I worked with set up a system to encourage his employees to take incoming service calls, which is not a popular activity. These engineers would much rather be digging into complex software problems or writing new programs than answering phones. The leader proposed that for every five hours logged on the customer service portal, a technician earns one hour at the end of the month to devote to his or her own special projects.

The manager reframed the activity as a reward system. Rather than seeing helpline calls as distractions pulling them away from cool projects, the engineers now see these tasks as a way to enable more work time on projects they enjoy.

You can also set your Masters to work on some of the long-range projects your organization needs to thrive five, ten, or even fifty years from today. Projects such as research, new product development, or theorycrafting strategy are a good fit for the gritty geek. If a task aligns with their CoG, chances are the geek will stick with it, and you, until the end.

The CoG also plays a role in the process of learning and development. We had the opportunity to chat with Sam Swords, a medieval combat enthusiast, actor, filmmaker, and European martial artist. Sam writes a successful blog and has worked on and off-screen for movies such as *The Hobbit* trilogy and *X-Men: Dark Phoenix.*

During our interview, Sam shared a secret project he was working on. It was a new gauntlet designed to allow a greater range of movement while offering full protection to the sword hand. He developed a prototype of this armored glove in collaboration with a friend who designs movie props. To really make the glove effective Sam first had to learn more about the crafting process.

Studying up on science and engineering materials allowed Sam to contribute his ideas to the project. His motivation to pursue this project is easy to understand. If you create the best equipment you win more sword fights. A rewarding byproduct for his work towards this goal was that he learned new engineering skills along the way.

As a business leader, consider engineering some learning opportunities of your own. Can you build professional development plans into a project your employees can geek out on?

If you have a team of entry-level marketing analysts who happen to be fantasy sports fanatics, starting a league might encourage them to learn the calculations behind the competition. If understanding how to make projections based on a data set helps your employee win their next head-to-head match in the league, they may not pause to be intimidated by the math involved.

QUESTIONS TO CONSIDER

1. Have you discovered the geeks you need to achieve your team's goals? Where might you start looking to find untapped pools of talent who geek on what you do?

2. How can you ask better interview questions to reveal the Centers of Gravity of candidates?

3. What is one simple way you could garner more feedback and insights from the geeks in your workforce or customer base?

4. What are you doing to keep the geeks in your team connected to the work they love or connecting what they love to the work?

5. How can you connect important learning for your employees to their passions and interests?

MEET A GEEK 2: BARISTAS

When you imagine a barista, what do you picture? Perfectly coiffed hair? A quirky personality or tattooed arms? Maybe you have never thought past the warm beverage you are receiving to the person who crafted it.

The barista at your local cafe may appear to be like any other restaurant worker but the task they are performing is anything but ordinary. As one barista put it, "You are working with something that is more chemically complex than almost anything else that we imbibe as a human being." Another describes coffee as "so difficult that chefs won't even touch it."

Since the rise of a large, Seattle-based corporation in the 1960s, a new wave of coffee consumption has been born. Coffee has been transformed from a commodity into an artisanal product like wine or scotch.

Just as a winemaker must consider the flavor combinations in their glass of pinot noir, a barista must understand the different elements that comprise a particular cup of espresso. The manner in which some of these craftspeople deliver coffee knowledge is akin to a watching a passionate preacher deliver a sermon.

Perfection is the end goal, and what better way to test the level of perfection a barista can achieve than to enter a barista competition? Yes, you read that correctly: a coffee competition.

For skilled coffee makers, these competitions transcend the usual Starbucks experience and enter a whole new world of caffeinated flavor and creativity.

We talked with Todd, the 2014 US Brewers Cup Champion, about how he got his start in competitions. He explains, "I have been working in the coffee industry for over 15 years now. I started drinking coffee in junior high, drinking it black. For me, it has always just been about trying better and better coffee."

In college, Todd spent a lot of time studying at coffeehouses. It just made sense that his first job would be at the local Starbucks. His motivation? "Employees get free drinks, so..."

Todd quickly became known as *the* coffee person; anyone in his life with a question about caffeinated beverages came to him. Todd had the answers. He could spout the entire coffee supply chain, from farm to cup. He understood each step of the process completely. In fact, Todd even began leading tastings and discussions for his fellow employees at the cafe.

He remembers his first time at a barista competition. "I was a district manager in Hollywood in 2009. There was a flier in the back of one of my stores about a barista competition that was happening. It was [taking place] across the street from one of my stores.

I had some time so I went that Friday afternoon. I walked into the warehouse and I was kind of dumbfounded with what was going on in front of me. I had no idea this side of coffee existed. Starbucks call themselves specialty coffee, but this was a whole other side of it. I thought it was very cool so I hung out for a few hours. I got to experience the whole thing."

Let's discuss the particulars of competing. The World Barista Competition involves a 15-minute service routine in which three rounds of drinks are prepared for a panel of judges. Each competitor is evaluated by four sensory judges, two technical judges, and one head judge. In this short period of time, 12 drinks must be concocted and seven judges wowed.

The order of drinks is the same for everyone: first round is espresso, then cappuccino, then the presentation of a signature drink. The signature drink is a creative and personal espresso beverage made with any ingredients the competitor wishes to use. This final round is a chance for each barista to showcase skill and artistry.

During these 15 minutes, the competitor will be judged on service, creativity, and precision. Points are deducted for any small misstep, including wiping a stray hair from your face, forgetting to clean off the machine, or allowing a beverage to drip onto the judges' table.

How stiff is the competition? In 2015, one thousand baristas competed to enter the U.S. Barista Competition. Only 41 actually made it to the national stage.

These craftspeople practice their routines for months and months at a time until the act flows as easily as a choreographed dance. The preparation regimens are intense. One competitor explained that, in order to learn its complexity, she drank a particular coffee for so many days on end that after the competition she looked at the beverage and was physically ill.

Another competitor mentioned sleeping next to his machine at night in order to become one with it. He borrowed this practice from ancient Japanese warriors. Sleeping next to their weapons was thought to allow these warriors to establish a connection between their hand and the blade the moment it was picked it up. The fighter was able to lose his inhibitions and unconsciously perform at a higher level.

Scott, a third-place winner of the U.S. Barista Competition, 2009 Great Lakes Regional Winner, and Co-Owner and Manager of Kickapoo Coffee in Milwaukee, has 14 years of experience in the coffee business.

Like Todd, Scott's beginnings in the coffee business were unplanned. "My getting a job at a cafe was unintentional. I actually considered food service below the standard I held for myself. I had previously worked at an animal shelter and was born and raised on a farm. I had preconceived notions about working in food service and thought that it would be boring and unfulfilling. I had gone seven months without a job, was sick of waiting, and desperate."

After enough time, Scott was hooked on coffee service. He found it fulfilling to be part of the barista community, even if he thought some of the other competitors could be a little over the top at times. Eventually, he was clued-in to the world of competitive coffee making.

"I realized that barista competitions were the venue for those baristas who believed they were exceptional or that the coffee they worked with was exceptional. I wanted to get close to that just to see if I may have had anything in common."

His company would not sponsor him to attend a competition as a spectator. In order to go, he would need to be the one competing. Scott was not ready yet. He told us, "a few years later I learned that I could pursue a judge's training to judge a barista competition. I got my employers to agree to support me in going to the 2006 United States Barista Competition in Charlotte, NC.

About three minutes into my first round of judging I knew I had what it took to be a competitor. That year I started mentally, and later physically, preparing for the next year's barista competition."

Scott felt very strongly about marrying his passion with his vocation. He could not come to work every day and leave his CoG at the door. "My passion for coffee and working in coffee has made me make the conscious decision that my work life would also be my personal life. I did not want to lead separate lives." As manager and co-owner of his very own cafe, Scott has found the balance.

Each day, he continually pushes himself to remain innovative in a very by-the-book industry. "I often wanted to break rules that existed in my cafe, rules I thought were unnecessary and may even slow me down, whether it be to say this way is better than that way, or this technique is better than that technique." He is continuously improving and reinventing the way coffee is made.

When a barista shares with someone that they make coffee for a living the response can be a certain degree of judgment or doubt that the job can be fulfilling. The competitive world of coffee proves these naysayers wrong. The craft involves a high level of mastery in both knowledge and technique.

MASTERS TO MAKERS

Once you have researched, observed, cataloged, memorized, visualized, and debated every possible angle of the final season of *Battlestar Galactica*, what is left? Writing fan fiction of course! The drive to create is a natural next step for Masters. You turn inward, looking at the knowledge, skills, and abilities you have developed in pursuit of your passion, and set out to *make* something all your own.

PART
MAKERS
2

MEET A GEEK 3: SCULPTOR

Humans have always been Makers. The Statue of Liberty, Great Sphinx of Giza, and Statue of David in Florence are famous works that most of us can readily call to mind. Now, can you tell me *who* created them?

David was crafted by Michelangelo; That is a fairly easy one. Congratulations if you knew Gustave Eiffel built the Statue of Liberty, and double bonus points if you knew it was designed by sculptor Frédéric Auguste Bartholdi.

But how about the Sphinx? Trick question. A huge debate still remains as to when, why, and for whom it was built it. Thousands of years old, the mystery of the Sphinx still remains today.

Many sculptures have outlived and outshone the artists who have created them. Kim, a modern day sculptor of fantasy creations, explains the beauty of crafting something bigger than yourself. "You get to make something that lasts, that will live past you, and that has the potential to become an icon of that culture, like the Parthenon in ancient Greece. Literature is a gift to the future, but artwork identifies the culture. I like the idea that I am becoming a part of history."

Kim's thoughts shed some light on how Makers are inspired. Besides being aesthetically pleasing, art from centuries past tells us about the behaviors, the appearance, and the values a culture once held. Man-made artifacts found at an archaeological dig can rewrite history books and forever change the way we think about the past.

Kim lived in an environment where invention was encouraged. "I grew up in rural Montana, where farm kids could build anything, and we did! I was always thinking to myself, 'What is a new tool to build with?' Influenced by my lumberjack father, I was a hyperactive kid always focused on something."

When she began looking for a job, Kim knew she wanted to do something hands-on. This led her to work as a housekeeper in Seattle for 12 years before she was injured and had to quit. Work most of us would complain about, Kim did not want to leave cleaning because the thought of working a desk job and sitting around all day was more than she could bear.

This time of transition was an opportunity for her to pursue something different. "I didn't settle into a job, I kept on learning. I have always loved art. Most children have a love of fairies and magical creatures at a young age, but then they shift that focus to being passionate about real animals. I didn't. No one in Montana was interested in fantasy. It wasn't until I turned 25 that I found a tribe of others who shared my interest and gave me the validation I needed.

What I really wanted to do was bring fantasy to the real world, but how could I do that? It took me seven years to figure it out. I had to learn on my own how to work with molds, how to cast my work, and how to make large hollow sculptures."

Kim spent upwards of $700,000 learning to sculpt. Building tools and materials were expensive! When she built a four foot tall dragon statue, she burned through about a half a ton of clay.

For 17 years Kim spent her days producing large props for companies, such as the large Santas you see in craft stores. Creating these pieces brought in money but was not rewarding work. In her spare time, Kim was still sculpting fantasy pieces.

Her work and her art remained separate. "My skills exist separately from the profitable art I make. That side of me is a separate entity. Inside me is my art, but I also have to do what is good for business. My fire is my artwork." How could she better align her work with her CoG?

Inspired to create a safer and cheaper material to build with, Kim tried her hand at inventing a new sculpting material. With the help of her husband, who had patiently listened to her complaints every time she suited up in hazmat gear to open a package of toxic sculpting material, the two spent 14 months on product development.

Kim spoke candidly about the process of creation. "I burned up money on testing, but geeks don't give up! The hunt is the most fun. People who are passionate are not always happy, but they are driven and motivated to achieve the results no one else can."

After enough testing, finally, Pal Tiya was brought to the market. This material would allow Kim and countless others to pursue and discover a passion for sculpting.

Kim explains the opportunity her clay brings. "To learn sculpting people need a lot of money and materials to pursue the craft, but the question remains: Will you make a profit off your work? I feel that it is unethical [to teach such an art]. With the new material I was able to develop, the burden of cost is no longer the case."

Pal Tiya has many fans, one of which is Sir Richard Taylor, five-time Academy Award Winner and founder of Weta Workshop, a special effects and prop company based in New Zealand that produces effects for television and film.

The company has worked on over 60 feature films, some of which include: *The Lord of the Rings Trilogy*, *King Kong*, *The Chronicles of Narnia*, *Avatar*, *The Hobbit Trilogy*, *The Amazing Spider-Man 2*, and *Godzilla*.

Weta Workshop describes itself as having the necessary resources and tools to "create anything from hand-made weapons, costuming, makeup effects and creature suits through to full-scale tanks, aircraft, miniatures of any scale and vehicle construction." And thanks to Kim's invention, the creative process of the countless artists who work here creating fantasy art is being accelerated.

Richard and Kim come from similar backgrounds. Growing up in a rural area, Richard was taught creativity at a young age. In his words, he grew up in a "sheddy culture, where your father builds everything out of a shed. He had built our car, our boat, our furniture. And then he and I and my mum spent five years building our family home."

It was his upbringing, rather than a formal training in fine arts, that led to his success in the film industry. His passion for fantastical art became a career that would eventually spark the careers of other artists and transform films as we know them.

Before he was able to do all that, Richard began his work sculpting in a hotel kitchen. His first sculptures were made out of margarine and displayed on the buffet table during meals.

As a young artist, Richard had not yet invested his time into material research, nor did he have the money to do so. "The reason I sculpted margarine was that my knowledge was minimal. I had little knowledge of other available materials, so margarine suited my requirements. I'd sculpt dragons, giants, trolls and bird men; all sorts of crazy things. I'd get paid in food."

Today, Kim works in the Weta Workshop creating pieces to educate a new generation of sculptors. On her company blog, there are step-by-step tutorials of her team at Weta sculpting miniature villages out of Pal Tiya clay.

When she set out to invent a new type of sculpting material Kim was just trying to protect her health and improve her craft. Today, Pal Tiya helps Kim create the art she enjoys and connects her to a community of like-minded geeks who share in the same passion.

MAKERS: THE CoG IS THE MOTHER OF INVENTION

In the late 1990s in Little Chute, Wisconsin, a boy named Richard Schepp was born 12 weeks premature and the lone survivor of triplets. Early in his time at the Neonatal Intensive Care Unit, it was discovered Richard had an intracranial bleed that would cause him distress for the rest of his life. Richard is hydrocephalic, and because of problems with the fluid system in his brain, pressure continuously builds in his skull, putting his life at risk.

Modern medicine addresses this condition by utilizing a shunt. This is literally a hole drilled in the skull to relieve pressure when cerebrospinal fluid does not disperse properly. Shunts can sometimes fail, allowing pressure in the skull to build to dangerous levels. The symptoms of this failure would start out minor issues like headaches and nausea.

When my son Gabe has a headache or feels nauseous, I give him some Tylenol and put him to bed. The Schepps had to take more care, as any of these seemingly innocent symptoms could be a sign of looming catastrophe, a warning that the shunt was not functioning properly. Even the smallest problem had to be addressed as if it had the potential to be life-threatening.

Living two hours away from the nearest hospital that could support their son's needs, Richard's parents were regularly faced with an anxiety-ridden race to the emergency room to check his shunt. This is not a simple or painless procedure. Every time the headaches struck, Richard was wheeled into surgery for inspection and correction of the device. Richard spend most of his first three years on this earth in the hospital. For chronically ill children and their families life can be painful, expensive, and exhausting.

Decades before Richard was born, another little boy grew up pursuing a very specific geeky interest. Saving up his allowance money he purchased a Commodore 64, one of the earliest models of the personal computer. I remember using this very same platform to play classic video games like *Archon*, *Pirates!*, and *Ultima IV.* Little Josh Medows, on the other hand, used the C64 to teach himself computer programming.

In his spare time throughout high school, college, medical school, and into the start of his career, Josh played around with computers. He eventually became a physician at the University of Wisconsin-Madison health system, in the very hospital where Richard Schepp received treatment. Dr. Medows was exposed to the trauma and heartache of the Schepp family and others like them on a daily basis. Going home each night with those experiences in his mind, Josh tapped into his geeky passion to find a solution.

In his basement, Dr. Medows had a fully equipped computer science workshop: *a geek's dream*. This was the place he would go to immerse himself in his CoG. He experimented on and improved various pet projects to ease the suffering of the patients he cared for each day.

One such project emerged after he started working with kids like Richard. The result of this project was the Intracranial Pressure (ICP) Monitor. This monitor detects pressure building in the fluid of the skull and allows physicians to diagnose the cause of these symptoms *without surgeries.*

The first prototype Dr. Medows created was almost as large as a pizza box. The device functioned, but it was obviously of little use if it did not fit inside the cranium. Dr. Medows took a bold step. He brought his rudimentary prototype to other scientists in the UW-Madison health system, asking for their feedback and advice.

I say bold because it takes guts for an amateur Maker to present something he has assembled in his basement to a group of professional scientists and ask for feedback. Imagine you were a proud, successful attorney who also happened to write short stories as a hobby. How might you feel if I asked you to bundle some of those stories up, the ones you have never shared with anyone except close friends, and send them to several published authors for feedback? If you are anything like me, the answer is terrified.

Dr. Medows' boldness paid off. The team of engineers and physicians were intrigued by his idea and jumped in to help. Together, they managed to create an ICP monitor smaller than a pinky nail. The monitor can be implanted in the skull, allowing physicians to measure pressure readings remotely by simply waving a receiver over a child's head. No more surgery. No more needles. No more unnecessary pain and fear for children and their parents. Richard Schepp was one of the first kids to receive a monitor and it changed his life, and the life of his family, forever.

I love the story of Richard Schepp and Dr. Medows because it is the tale of a geeky kid who grew up and found a way to leverage his Center of Gravity to create something important. He recognized the ability his obsessive interest had granted him and he put its power to good use.

Many are searching for new answers to old problems, but few of us have the energy or dedication to doggedly pursue a solution. Organizations struggle in the same way. It is exhausting to overcome challenges or disrupt established practices and become truly innovative. There are endless resources, tools, and experts purportedly helping us drive innovation and achievement, but I would argue that the real key to overcoming these obstacles is identifying and leveraging your internal drivers. A driver can be a person or an idea that is persistent enough to get you to where you want to be.

INNOVATIVE GEEKS

In my experience as a leadership development consultant, I cannot tell you how many times I have heard an executive leader discuss how critical innovation is to the success of his business. And yet, so many organizations stumble down the same path as now-defunct Blockbuster Video, failing to make the creative leap in order to stay alive. Even more common, though less spectacular, are the businesses who grind along producing the same product, the same way, for decades, missing big opportunities because "If it ain't broke…"

I strongly believe that most organizations' failure to innovate is caused by a fundamental misunderstanding of the concept. When leaders talk about innovation what they are frequently describing is the conceptualization of something entirely new, or *invention*. They want to see a bold, disruptive technology emerge and redefine the industry, e.g. their iPhone moment.

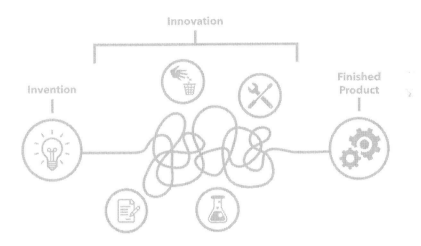

While an enticing goal in its own right, invention is not innovation. Innovation is the process of taking a new idea and turning it into a finished, working product. Essentially, innovation encapsulates everything occurring *after* the moment of invention…so, the hard part.

Back in middle school I sketched an idea on a sheet of graph paper one lunch period. My invention? A car with small generators attached to each wheel that could create electricity to charge the battery during braking.

Years later, I remember seeing the fully realized idea of regenerative braking in *Popular Mechanics* and thinking,

"Aww man, that was my idea!" But of course it was not. I gave up on the idea moments after I invented it. I did not have the sustaining hunger to complete a true work of innovation.

I think a lot of us have these moments. What ideas have you left sitting on a legal pad, white board, or bar napkin that now belong to someone else because that person actually had the drive to take it to the finish line?

We can learn a lot about innovation from the geeky Maker. Passion is a driver that pushes the geek past simple invention to delivery of a finished product. Not all geeks create to solve life-threatening issues like Dr. Medows did. Makers are perhaps more similar to artists than they are to engineers. Their innovations are typically born of appreciation or pride rather than necessity. But even these less pragmatic catalysts of innovation create items of interest and utility.

Geeks become Makers for a variety of reasons. Understanding these drivers can help us motivate ourselves and others to innovate and create the solutions we need.

1.) Geeks Create to Gain Ownership of their CoG

If you are not a gamer you are probably unfamiliar with mods. These are extensions of preexisting video games created by fans wanting to play the game in a different way. I might create a mod to make the main character in a game resemble my favorite talk show host, change the soundtrack to include music from my friend's punk band, or add an entire new area or level of the game world to explore. Gaming geeks create mods out of a desire to make the game their own, a process of personalization that often requires hundreds of hours of coding and testing.

In these cases the act of creation brings the geek closer to the thing he loves. It provides him with a sense of ownership to see something he created living alongside or within his CoG.

I recently took up playing *Dungeons & Dragons* again, this time as the Dungeon Master. Instead of purchasing a pre-written adventure, I have been writing my own homebrew campaign in collaboration with my players. I have never been so excited. The sense of pride that comes from incorporating my own ideas and creations into something I already love makes a significant difference in my enjoyment of the game.

2.) Geeks Create to Prove They Can

In his book *iWoz*, Steve Wozniak describes how he cultivated the skills needed to create the early computer system that was the foundation for the Macintosh computer.

He recalls, "Many times I'd redesign the same computer a second or third time, using newer and better components. I developed a private little game of trying to design these minicomputers with the minimum number of chips. I have no idea why this became the pastime of my life. I did it all alone in my room with my door shut. It was a private hobby. I didn't share this activity with my parents, friends, teachers, or anyone over the years."

Steve felt driven to build just to prove to himself that he could build it better, faster, and simpler than every time before. This drive to excel also drives geek Masters. The geek is drawn back into action again and again, subtly influenced by the simple desire for improvement. The result of this patient experimentation is sometimes breakthrough innovation.

3.) Geeks Create to Remove Obstacles

Innovation is often driven by scarcity or adversity. Geeks who cannot bear the thought of being separated from their passion will invest real effort to discover a way to make it possible despite the obstacles.

Some geeks create in order to carve out more space for involvement in their CoG. Remember Kim, the sculptor who loved her craft so much that it was *literally* killing her? Many of the materials she used to make her art were toxic but she simply could not quit sculpting.

The new sculpting clay Kim invented allowed her to improve her art and remove the risk. At the same time, she improved the craft for thousands of other sculptors.

4.) Geeks Create to Share their CoG

Sharing is often the impetus of geek artists. They create to expose others to the joy of their Center of Gravity. Knitters used to spend hours buying books, talking to others in the community, and hunting through the yarn store to find their next pattern. Now crafting an amazing scarf, baby blanket, or stuffed Chewbacca toy is as easy as logging into Pintrest.

Knitting geeks are publishing their own patterns at little to no cost on websites like Ravelry and allfreeknitting.com. Creating a knitting pattern takes a lot of effort. The pattern starts with a concept, then is tested and revised, and finally documented online.

Why are knitting geeks putting in dozens of hours only to place these patterns online at no cost for the world to use? The motive is simple. Knitters want to know that a fellow artisan is experiencing the same joy they had while making the pattern. I have a motive when I coerce my friends into sitting down to watch the full run of the *Battlestar Galactica* reboot. Although I did not produce, write, or act in that show myself, I still feel a powerful desire to share the love.

Innovation is frequently a combination of passion-driven creativity and obsession-fueled determination. In the same way geeks master complex skills, taking a new idea and turning it into something concrete and useful takes patience and enthusiasm.

GEEKS IN SHINING ARMOR

Remember the chain mail armor my cousin was working on? As a reminder of just what a demanding project that truly was, I made the attempt myself recently. With the help of two friends I spent time crafting a paltry 3-inch square, maybe two percent of a complete shirt. *It took me hours.* During high school and college, Chris created four full unique suits. Not to mention a few headpieces and sets of gauntlets. The sheer volume of work required to craft these pieces is staggering.

Even after hundreds of hours invested, Chris still considers himself a rank amateur compared to a group of craftspeople and competitors known as the Knights of the Serpent. This elite group is part of a larger organization called Amtgard, a global assembly of medieval combat enthusiasts with over 50,000 members. While most members of Amtgard admire, purchase, and regularly use these kinds of armor and weapons in mock combat, only a select few take on the role of artisan.

Have you ever been to a state or county fair? In one large tent you can find a competitive fair exhibit wherein quilts, pies, or butter sculptures are judged to select a blue ribbon winner. Replace these objects in your mind with longswords, helmets, and suits of gleaming armor and you now have some idea of what you would find at an Amtgard Arts & Sciences Tournament.

The range of skills is vast. You might see a 13-year-old kid displaying his first leather jerkin alongside a calloused veteran showing off a matched set of gemstone-adorned steel scale armor.

To win a local or state contest in this community requires a measure of talent and obsession, but the Knights of the Serpent are on another level in the world of Amtgard. To be invited to join this elite group, one must demonstrate crafting skill by wining awards at the highest levels as many as *ten* times. Talent like this requires a champion-level investment of time honing the craft. The results are spectacular. Just Google it. Trust me you will not be disappointed.

These craftspeople are Makers in the purest sense, creating beautiful art from metal, sweat, and *love*. The geeks around you are driven in a similar way.

USE THE FORCE

How can you drive innovation and productivity with Geek power?

If you are a leader who wants to inspire innovation, consider the environment a geek needs in order to feel engaged enough to create. You cannot force innovation. Invite it insteas by removing the most common barriers and getting out of the way.

Organizational team leaders can tap into the power of geeks to increase productivity and innovation. Both outcomes are driven in part by employee engagement, the state in which an employee is energized and committed to his or her work.

Essentially engagement is your employees geeking out on their jobs. Not simply job satisfaction, employee engagement refers to more than just tolerance of the work and workplace. It is about passion that drives the bottom line. According to the

Gallup State of the American Workplace Report, companies with high employee engagement exhibit 22 percent higher levels of productivity than their counterparts. Engaged workplaces also experience dramatically lower turnover, absenteeism, and health outcomes as a result of increased employee engagement.

Engaged employees are more likely to seek new ways to innovate, whether this means improving customer experience, cutting costs, building the brand, or improving performance quality. Engagement is essential to the health of a successful organization, which is why companies spend vast amounts of time and money trying to understand on improving it.

Again, I argue employee engagement is just a term for people who geek out on the job. What companies are really striving for is a way to grant employees the *permission* to geek out on work. You cannot force engagement, but you can remove the barriers employees face in achieving engagement. Leaders should strive to create a work environment where potential geeks feel supported and confident enough to pursue their passions publicly, without fear of judgment or retribution.

In my work with organizational leaders I teach several key drivers of engagement. Addressing the following questions can help you and your team gauge where you currently stand and how you can improve on the drivers of engagement: safety, connection, recognition, and fulfillment. How would your employees or team members answer these? How would you? Where do the differences in the two answers lie?

1.) Safety

- Can I share criticism or concern without fear of retribution?

- Am I able to share ideas without worry that a failure will be permanently attached to my reputation?

- Do I feel secure enough in my role and in my organization to focus on my work rather than a passive job search?

2.) Connection

- Am I plugged into the necessary processes, information, and people I need to empower my work?

- Do I understand organization-level strategy and see the role I play in the achievement of key business objectives?

- Am I familiar with and understand my colleagues' and my shared purpose?

3.) Recognition

- Do I feel my work is valued and not just a side project, cost center, or afterthought?

- Do my leaders and colleagues recognize my worth and the effort I put forth each day?

- Is my innovative behavior rewarded, or dismissed as inefficient or out-of-scope?

4.) Fulfillment

• Am I able to perform job tasks that align with my strengths?

• Do I feel that I am making progress and achieving success?

• Is my work challenging or am I bored at my desk?

• Is my work aligned with my personal values?

• Do I care about what we are doing as an organization?

Let me be clear, these four drivers do not magically create engagement where the potential does not already exist. Engagement drivers enable the potential. Not everyone is getting in the car and driving to their dream job tomorrow, nor does every role offer the same potential for engagement. Business leaders should acknowledge 100 percent engagement is a pipe dream. Even though we won't reach everyone at that level, we shouldn't give up on engaging employees!

Year after year, researchers find that more than half of the American workforce is disengaged. You can move the needle! As leaders, we cannot create engagement out of thin air. We cannot always change the work itself. We cannot always change the people doing the work. We can change the culture and climate of our workplaces by adjusting our own leadership style. We can influence drivers of engagement. Our focus belongs here if we want to be successful leaders of productivity and innovation.

Lift barriers by teaching managers to have real conversations with employees. Focus your attention on relationship building, listening techniques, and transparent communication. Depending on your corporate culture, integrating new behaviors may be difficult, so start small. Work to improve the habits of immediate team members first, then move onto other teams. Geeks are just waiting to be empowered, in your office, in your stores, and in your factories. Let them model the kinds of attitudes and behaviors you want to see in your culture.

Geeks need to be given the room and resources to run with their ideas. Once your culture is focused on driving employee engagement, the ability to promote and nurture innovative ideas becomes much easier. Crafting a workplace supporting "pursuit of passion" behavior increases management's access to the reservoir of potential energy in the company's talent pool.

If you expect geeks to take you at your word when you say "take risks, try new things, innovate," it is up to you to make people feel safe enough to act in these ways.

Consider a comic book store, with its rows and rows of the latest releases, boxes of plastic-wrapped collectibles, and game tables popped up in the back waiting for someone to strike up a match of *Magic the Gathering*. Do not be fooled. The comic store is not just a retail establishment. It is as much a community hub as the sports bar or dog park.

Many of the comic book geeks we interviewed mentioned their local shop as a place of safety, a place they frequented because they knew they would not be judged for the things they liked. This safe environment empowered them to try new things, even share their thoughts and opinions with others. The aisles of new books offer opportunities to strike up conversations with fellow geeks. Many times these interactions will result in a recommendation to try out a new story. As I met these folks, I was led to read dozens of comics that I would never have reached for on my own, all because of an impassioned pitch from a fan. Sounds like a recipe for innovation to me.

What can you do as a leader to create that same feeling of safety and collaboration in the workplace? Many innovative companies now allow time for their employees to tinker and create. Leaders at 3M, makers of brands like Scotch tape, are often credited with creating the idea of *15 percent time*, the mandate for 3M engineers to invest 15 percent of each week into working on self-interest projects. Self-directed and supported with company resources, the outcomes these geeks are able to produce with their time pay huge dividends. Google claims some of its most valuable products, apps like AdSense and Gmail, have resulted from a similar program the company cleverly titled *20 percent time*.

Many organizations talk a big game about innovation. In my professional experience, I have learned the easiest way to understand what a company actually values is to watch where money is spent and note which behaviors are being rewarded.

Look at your organization's policies and leader behaviors and ask yourself some potentially tough questions. Is my company recognizing and reinforcing innovation behaviors like collaboration, autonomy, and risk taking? Do we put our money behind this message by budgeting time and treasure to empower our people? How do we react to innovation when it deviates from the norms to which we have become accustomed? For example, when a customer service rep in your call center spends an afternoon setting up a comfortable space for their team to decompress after a difficult call, is their manager supportive of testing it out? Or are new ideas like this met with encouragement to get back to work?

Real innovation is a product of focused, collaborative, iterative, and supported work. Geeks will sign up for this work when it aligns with their CoG, and so will others within your organization will if the environment is right.

QUESTIONS TO CONSIDER

1. Which of the four drivers of engagement could your organization or team benefit the most from improving? Safety, connection, recognition, or fulfillment?

2. What can you do in your role to improve that driver?

3. Do your employees have a comic book store equivalent, a safe hub for collaboration and idea sharing? How could you build one or equip them to build one?

4. Are there cultural norms holding your organization back from real innovation or stifling the sort of thinking that makes it possible?

MEET A GEEK 4: BEEVANGELISTS

Charlie has led an unconventional life. He took his background in marketing and design and decided to apply them to his true calling in life: *honey bees*.

We asked him, "why bees?" Charlie replied, "When you look back through time, a great number of people who have been beekeepers have been influential in the world as we know it. Aristotle was a beekeeper; He figured out life on earth and how we get along in civilizations looking in on a beehive."

In 2003, Charlie moved away from corporate life in favor of non-profit work. After a career at Apple he joined the marketing team at Growing Power and the Michael Fields Agricultural Institute, where he caught the buzz for beekeeping.

It was soon after that he fell on hard times. "The bank foreclosed on the house and life got to be really sparse, but it didn't matter because I was just doing bee stuff. I was known all over as 'the bee guy.'"

During his work for the bees, he came across four nuns who were aspiring beekeepers from a tiny village in Wisconsin. Without the correct resources, these women were unable to start a hive. Charlie decided he needed to make beekeeping possible for everyone, and so he began his work improving the future of urban beekeeping.

Of the process he says, "When you're an industrial designer, you're always looking for something that hasn't changed in a long time. The beehive hasn't changed in 150 years. In 2006 when colony collapse started to happen, with the knowledge that I felt I had gained in understanding the personalities of bees, the idea of trying to find a solution was paramount. 2002 to 2009 were failed attempts at doing it right, which were all the obsession of perfecting it. There were times we felt we could save the world."

The new beehive that Charlie created was modeled after naturally occurring hives from around the world. The layout of the new hive made collecting honey less stressful for the bees, increased the yield, and calmed the bees so they were easier to handle.

This invention was much more than just a product; it was a mission. Educating consumers about the importance bees play in our ecosystem was vital to selling the hive. Charlie could not provide the product without first explaining its significance.

Charlie teaches communities about sustainability and fosters a greater appreciation for bees and beekeeping. His beepods are manufactured in Wisconsin and sold across North America. He has non-profit training centers located at Boerner Botanical Gardens, Milwaukee's Urban Ecology Centers, community farm cooperatives, universities, backyards, and the rooftops of high-rise office buildings.

Charlie calls his community of fellow beekeepers the Beevangelists. The group is on a mission to help nature's principle pollinators find success in crazy times. Through advocacy and education they work to *Bee the Change!*

The disappearance of the honey bee is a crisis widely

covered by new outlets today. As consumers we better understand why bees are needed to continue food production. What is not as widely understood is how modern agricultural practices are aiding in their demise.

Charlie shared that as farms became corporate, people believed that bigger was better. In addition to larger production farms becoming the norm, there was also a trend towards monoculture, growing only one type of crop in an area. Charlie pointed out that without a variety of plant life to support them, insects living on such farm will not thrive.

He believes that rather than growing bigger fields, moving bees to backyards is a better plan. Bees like biodiversity and a typical neighborhood has dozens of varieties of trees, shrubs, and flowers. This approach stems from a new mindset - that beekeeping is less about honey and all about food.

Charlie went on to explain that the very adaptations that have allowed bees to prosper for so long are leading to their downfall. "Bees rapidly advance and mutate, this is what they have been doing for 180 million years. The very mutation DNA that's in a bee is causing it to die faster. They are evolving to understand diesel fumes, neonicotinoids, mono-culture. How do we fix that?

If we get these hives to be as ubiquitous as fire hydrants and if we can get neighborhoods to care about them as much as they do as fire hydrants, we could have the world ready to fix agriculture. If human interaction is what is killing them, then let's make human interaction what might save them."

Charlie tried to patent his invention after he brought the hive to a trade show and received an overwhelming response. A year later, he learned that once a product was introduced to the public the inventor only has two years to secure a patent and claim the intellectual property. One year was already up. He had to move fast.

Working with a patent specialist, Charlie learned that he would have to pay $10,000 to secure the patent. But the specialist quickly racked up fees and by the time the bills had climbed to over $22,000, Charlie was too far in debt to continue. He declared the patent a lost cause. One of his collaborators bought him out and took over the brand.

Charlie described the failure to secure the patent as a blessing in disguise. Although the business was taken from him, Charlie continued to make products to support the bees. He didn't need a brand to do the work he loved. He continues to improve the invention and share it with the world, which was always his mission.

The loss of the company was a setback, but Charlie remains optimistic about the future. "I don't know how to turn it into a business model, but I can turn it into a *beevangelizing* model. I can get people to help for the love of it. Then it becomes how do we do it to be self-sustaining? How do we make it worth it to people? Do I charge $200 [to help with a hive] and have them feel unhappy but resolved, or do them a favor that makes them spread the buzz to three other people?"

Besides creating an amazing invention, Charlie has found success building a community of thousands of bee advocates. He is a true geek innovator using his geeky skills to recruit, train, and release environmental stewards into the community to tackle some of our earth's most pressing environmental issues.

MAKERS TO MISSIONARIES

Besides building products and services, geeks are also busy building unique communities. Do not underestimate how difficult and time-intensive this can be. The chairman of your local Bronie herd is likely investing 10-15 hours a week organizing, emailing, blogging, and recruiting. Not to mention engaging with members in person every day.

Niche communities are formed because geeks are Missionaries, passionate witnesses to the beauty of their CoG who love to share the love. Geeks are reaching out to the uninitiated, teaching others about their Center of Gravity, and building communities for others to share in their experiences. Geek Missionaries shape brands, engage members, and drive growth.

PART 3

MISSIONARIES

MEET A GEEK 5: BRONIES AND FANGIRLS

As human beings we feel a need to belong. We build communities in our cities, at our workplaces, or through our hobbies. With the help of the internet, community-builders are better able to find and connect people of similar interests across a larger geographic range. Niche groups amass large followings they might otherwise not have.

Thomas is a *Brony*, an obsessed fan of the show *My Little Pony: Friendship is Magic*. He is also the administrator of the U.S. Bronies Facebook page which has over 10,000 followers. We spoke with him to learn a little more about the community and how he became involved.

He explained how the show teaches men compassion, unlike the violent video games, movies, and television consumed by many. "The reason I watch My Little Pony is because of the morals. There is a strong undercurrent of friendship and positivity on the show."

As you might expect, the group receives a lot of negative criticism from outsiders. Our society has created norms and preconceived notions of masculinity. By becoming a Brony, these members are actively rejecting what they have been told a man should look like or how he should act.

Thomas acknowledges the judgment he faces as a Brony. "I think there has always been and probably always will be some negative connotations to the word simply because of the strangeness of a guy watching this show for the enjoyment of it. Obviously, it was a little weird at first, but I've always been a little off-center in my interests, wearing a pink tuxedo to the senior prom and all."

Why subject yourself to the scrutiny? The results of the 2014 State of the Herd Report, a study of over 20,000 Bronies conducted by a group of clinical psychologists, sheds some light. This community serves as a refuge for many of those who have suffered from bullying.

Support from the group helps members stand up to their bullies by instilling in them a newfound confidence. After joining the fandom, nearly half of those surveyed reported a decrease in verbal threats and physical attacks.

In addition, members who formerly avoided social situations found themselves seeking more chances to interact with others. Surveyed members also reported improved feelings of happiness and quality of life following membership. Bronies are a positive and supportive social group, as evidenced by the findings of this study.

Bronies are not the only stigmatized group, of course. Another community that few truly understand are fangirls. Alyssa was a Jonas Brothers fangirl "and will always be," as she told us. She is not alone in her fanaticism.

Alyssa described the legions of fangirls who sacrifice resources to prove love to a particular group. "Boy bands have been around for ages and women have always been obsessed with them. Even in everyday life we fantasize, picturing a first date in such detail before it even happens." Think the Beatles, Jackson 5, and the Backstreet Boys.

Although she enjoys the band's music, Alyssa's emotional connection to the Jonas Brothers goes far deeper than the songs. As a fangirl, Alyssa acts as a geeky Missionary.

She has invested countless hours researching minutiae of the Jonas Brothers' lives: if Nick was a crayon he would be Royal Blue, Kevin loves sushi and Thai food, Kevin's birthday is August 15, 1989. The list goes on.

If one could earn a Ph.D. in boy bands, Alyssa would be well on her way. She confessed to us that she once even baked a birthday cake for Nick Jonas and served it to a poster of him taped to her kitchen wall.

Perhaps the most interesting behavior we pulled from our interview with Alyssa was a compulsion to recruit fellow fangirls. She was always looking for opportunities to graffiti the Jonas Brothers' names or leave photos around town for others to find. "Whenever we would go out to eat I would always write JB with hearts surrounding it, along with the date, on the tablecloth, coaster, or kid menu. I would leave one of my drawings at the restaurant and make another one to take home with me. I had to leave my Jonas Brothers mark wherever I went, just to spread the word."

She could not justify this need. "There was no real reason behind what I did. I felt that I was on a constant journey of proving my loyalty." As their best fan, Alyssa felt it was her duty to share the Jonas Brothers experience with as many as possible.

Her friends were not exclusively other fangirls, but her best friend did share in Alyssa's passion with her. "[We] became obsessed with the Jonas Brothers around the same time. We ended up being known at school as 'The Jonas Brothers Girls' for carrying around their tote bags, having their posters, and going to every one of their concerts."

The Jonas Brothers were a popular band at the time Alyssa was growing up, but Alyssa's devotion was more extreme than many of her peers.

Others might not have understood why she acted the way she did. Why so obsessed over people you have never even met? Why make yourself a target for bullies? Her passion gave her a sense of purpose and connected her to friends that she might not otherwise have met, in person and online. "My devotion blinded me from anyone else's judgment. It didn't bother me in high school when people called me 'Jonas' because as a 16-year-old girl I was still carrying around a Jonas Brothers' tote bag.

Maybe these people were making fun of me, but I just thought 'Hey, that's my nickname.' I wore it as a badge of honor that I was a big enough of a fan that people noticed me. It just didn't make sense to me that you could not be obsessed with them. It's kind of like falling in love; You can't understand why other people can't see what you see in that person."

MISSIONARIES: MY NEAR-DEATH EXPERIENCE

I almost died dressed as a vampire in an airport hotel one winter evening. Before I tell you that story, let me give you some important context. You must first understand the difference between a Classic Role-Playing Game (RPG) and a Live Action Role-Playing (LARP) game.

Classic Role-Playing Games (RPGs)

Dungeons & Dragons is one of the oldest and best-known RPGs, but still hundreds more exist. RPGs are centered around storytelling. Each game is typically led by a narrator, known in *D&D* as the Dungeon Master. The narrator does not play a character, but is instead responsible for crafting and managing the world the characters are playing in. Dungeon Masters essentially play god in the adventure, an omnipotent being enforcing rules of play and unfolding the outcomes and consequences of each player's decisions.

Players, on the other hand, further the story by describing what their characters choose to do within the plot as it progresses. From swinging a sword to negotiating a peace treaty, the player orates his part of the story. Each character's choice impacts those of other players and the larger plot line, collaboratively determining the results of the game. Think of RPGs as *Choose Your Adventure* books, except vastly more complex since the decisions each player can make are not limited or made alone.

Picture the following interaction and you will have an accurate depiction of probably 80 percent of in-person, classic role-playing game scenarios:

A group of four friends gather in a basement or hobby shop back room around a card table piled high with salty snacks and caffeinated soft drinks. The Dungeon Master is positioned behind a small cardboard screen, hiding his notes and dice. One of the friends is always taking this far less seriously than the rest. Another player typically falls on the other end of the spectrum - hyper-enthusiastic about the adventure.

> **CHRIS (**Dungeon Master**):** "Roderick, the largest orc laughs at your efforts to intimidate him and then calls you a meek little gully dwarf" [*folds arms across chest and laughs mockingly*].

> **MATT (**Roderick**):** "I remove my Cloak of Inconvenient Pacifism and smite the orc with my Mithril battle axe" [*leans forward slightly, reaches for bag of Doritos*].

> **MIKE (**Findor**):** "I wander away from the fight to see if there are any chicks around. You guys are lame" [*snickers sarcastically, certain he is the coolest guy in this basement*].

> **CHRIS**: "Roderick, roll at least a 15 to strike the orc. Findor, you trip clumsily on Roderick's cloak and crack your pelvis."

These games are a ton of fun and involve a substantial

net caloric gain. I can recall weekends when we did not move from the table for almost 36 hours straight, except for bathroom breaks and snack refills. How can one nap when the fate of the kingdom hangs in the balance?

I know what you are thinking. This is all very interesting, but why were you in a hotel conference room dressed as a vampire? Let's talk about another level of role-playing geekiness.

Live Action Role-Playing Games (LARPs)

LARPs can be much more intense than RPGs. The most obvious difference between the two games is that players in a LARP do not stop at describing their character's actions. They will physically act them out. You can probably imagine some of the logistical differences immediately. The group needs enough space to make the world come to life in a physical way. A card table will not cut it when you need to swing a battle axe or dodge a punch. For this reason, LARP events often take place in very different settings than classic RPGs. You will find LARPers in hotels, convention halls, parking lots, and parks.

Like RPGs, each LARP has its own style. Some games are combat-heavy and emphasize the physical rules of mock fighting. Others dive deep into the theatrical side of the world and concentrate on costumes, conversations, and richly-detailed plot lines. A greater number of players may be required to run a LARP, as a pitched battle between two armies is hard to perform live on opposite sides of Picnic Area #3 without dozens of people armed to the tooth. LARP events require more resources than a neighbor's kitchen table can support.

Still confused? Here is an example. When a Wizard in your RPG wants to fry you with a Lightning Bolt spell she will tell you what she is doing, dramatically, one hopes, but she will just *say* it. When a Wizard in your LARP wants to zap you with a Lightning Bolt she might hold aloft a wooden rod topped with a shimmering crystal, cry out a series of Latin-sounding magic words, and throw glitter on you. One of these things is not like the other.

Now that you understand the fundamental differences between these two games, we can revisit my near-death vampiric encounter. Each January my chain mail-creating cousin and his wife visit Milwaukee from their home in Minneapolis. The primary purpose of the six-hour road trip is not to visit my wife and I, though we typically grab dinner or coffee while they are in town. The real reason for this journey is so the two can participate in the Midwinter Gaming Convention, a multi-day LARP event held downtown.

The couple is part of a LARP game called *Vampire: The Masquerade*. As I am sure you can guess from the title, this Gothic fantasy game involves players dressed up as vampires. For the Midwinter event, hundreds of players from around the Midwest take over a big hotel and conference center in full costume for a large format game lasting over two days. My wife and I refer to it as Vampire Weekend. The scale of this event would surprise many of those unfamiliar with the game, but it is not even the largest gathering of vampires, by a long shot.

Vampire is a global gaming organization with thousands of players across the U.S. and dozens of other countries. You may not have heard of it, but it is very popular. The plot lines span years, which requires players to adjust how a character behaves as it matures. Thirteen unique clans exist in *Vampire* and each player must choose one lineage to embrace and serve.

The *Vampire* world is robust and includes a fully functioning in-game government. If your character is successfully appointed the Sheriff of Cleveland, you have work to do in real life as well as within the game.

Walking into one of these events can feel as if you have stepped onto a movie set because of the staggering, lavish detail and care so many of these players pour into their clothing, hair, and make-up.

Business-minded vampires from the *Ventrue* clan strut past in Italian suits and tuxedos, not a single hair out of place, as befits the ruling class they represent. Grotesque packs of *Nosferatu,* a clan of vampire too hideous to pass as human, are easily spotted in their frightening makeup, looking like something out of your favorite horror flick. You might also see a lone *Malkavian,* a member of the clan of madness, wandering through the crowd and spouting mismatched lines of poetry and math problems to an invisible listener and wearing an outfit seemingly chosen by a lunatic in a thrift store.

On our first trip into this world we were wide-eyed and confused. *Vampire* is a deeply complex game for noobs to pick up. Luckily, my cousin plays a smooth-talking *Ventrue* capitalist and was only too happy to escort us around the cocktail hour. My near-death experience came when he formally introduced us to some of his in-game social network.

Before being pulled away to chat with another group of friends, Chris presented us to a woman whose costume I can only describe by asking you to imagine a movie-quality geisha with silk kimono, ebony hair pinned back in a tight bun, and carefully composed white facial make-up blended to perfection. Her character was an ancient Japanese vampire who greeted us with cold formality. We made polite conversation, until I misspoke. To be honest, I do not specifically recall what I said, but a moment later she was offended and threatening my life in a fit of rage. Carolyn and I were stunned, confused, and frantically looking around for an exit.

The geisha must have seen the bewildered look in my eyes because suddenly she relaxed, placed the two fingers of her right hand on her chest, and said with a big smile, "Oh, is this your first time playing?" She laughed, apologizing for the outburst. She explained why my question had been mortally offensive in this game to a vampire of her status.

After smoothing over the situation, she asked how our night was going and what our first impressions of the game were. She even offered to connect us with a local group of players. The geisha when on to explain the gesture she had been holding during our entire conversation, a sign to the rest of the players that we were "off-game," or not actively participating in the action at the moment. She told us to use this signal to call a time-out and ask a question or regain our bearings.

Had it not been for this brush with death and then subsequent warm welcome from an unexpected mentor, I very much doubt we would have returned to the game the following year. She put us at ease and actively welcomed us into her world.

Geeks like the *Vampire* geisha are Missionaries. The outpouring of love they feel for their Center of Gravity causes them to recruit new participants into their communities, deepen the engagement of current members, and build brand awareness among outsiders.

GEEK COMMUNITY BUILDERS

Geeks like my cousin Chris and the geisha reach out to those who might be interested in what they do, inviting these outsiders into the experience. In the introduction of this book, I mentioned that I travel the country to speak to different groups about my own geekiness. I am frequently approached by small groups of geeks as I come off stage.

Most of our conversations go something like, "It was really cool to hear you sharing your geeky stuff. Thanks for that. Now let me tell you all about *my* thing. You would love it!"

This never feels rude to me. Geeks do not mean to be self-centered when they talk on and on about what they love, they are simply unable to contain their genuine excitement. This is an opportunity to share their CoG with someone who they think might get it! One of the hardest parts of being a geek is trying to understand why the rest of the world is not as excited as you are about the latest movie trailer or fan fiction blog post, thinking *"How can they not see how amazing this is?!"*

Helping an outsider see the value of your CoG and converting them to the cause provides geeks with evidence to justify their own obsession. The combination of passion for the Center of Gravity and desire to be understood are powerful drivers that motivate geeks to act as Missionaries.

As we gathered research for this book we spoke to dozens of geeks of all stripes. One of the variables that remained constant across all conversations was my reaction to their enthusiasm. I found myself walking away from each interview thinking, *"That sounded really cool! I'd probably be into that."* Suddenly, I found myself looking up local Amtgard gatherings, shopping for backyard beehives, and reading new graphic novels outside my normal genres.

This reaction is less a symptom of my own propensity to geek out and more a result of the energy with which each geek talked about his or her CoG. Whether we were chatting with a fashion blogger or a coffee aficionado, geeks spoke of their interest with what one could only call true love. It felt almost like talking to my grandmother as she described her 60+ year love story with my grandpa. You cannot help but think, "I want that for myself." People with deep passions paint such a picture of satisfaction the affection is contagious.

T-SHIRT MEMBERS

In any organization or community, member engagement has a significant impact on culture and achievement of mission. My DECA chapter in high school had a group of what we referred to as t-shirt members.

Why did we call them this? Certain students signed up for the organization at the beginning of the year, paid their $10 dues, collected their DECA t-shirt, and were never to be seen again. They would add the organization to their resume and college applications, but that was just smoke and mirrors.

T-shirt members did not attend meetings or contribute to the chapter's goals, and so were essentially only members in title. For those of us who loved the organization, it became part of our mission to convert these members into true participants.

Geeks often engage the loosely involved by pulling them closer and closer into the heart of the community. Taking on the tasks of exposure, education, and encouragement of others, the geek's goal is to enrich the experience of all members in the community.

In my high school DECA chapter each member of the core leadership team committed his or her free time to mentoring two or three t-shirt members. The team personally invited these students to meetings, talked them through specific DECA activities we thought they might find interesting, and gently nudged them along until they had enough momentum to engage with the group on their own.

Stay or go, it was important to us t-shirt members had a real opportunity to love what we loved. It takes a direct and dedicated effort to pull these folks in from the periphery.

I've already mentioned one of my favorite geek Missionaries in this book - Charlie the beevangelist. When we first met, he was cupping something in his hands. He asked me to reach out and take whatever it was from him. As I got closer, I started to get pretty nervous. Charlie's hands were buzzing.

We were standing in a lush garden on the shores of Lake Michigan, in the heart of the St. Francis convent grounds, and all around me I could hear the buzzing. Tens of thousands of honeybees hovered and flitted among the apple trees, flower beds, and neat rows of vegetables. Charlie wanted me to reach out and hold one of those bees in my own hands! I hesitated, asking him some questions first in hopes that he was just kidding and would forget about this little prank. He could obviously sense my anxiety and distracted me by starting to talk about his work and his life.

Remember, Charlie is not just an inventor, he is a self-made expert and advocate for bees, especially in regards to their role in the global ecosystem and economy. Charlie has dedicated over a decade of his life to understanding bees and helping others do the same. In the face of a catastrophic collapse of hives around the world, his work is very relevant and important.

Charlie believes his work can shift mindsets and convince the public to view the insect more positively. He says, "Bees are stigmatized, and no one wants to be around them until we demystify them."

As he discussed this stigma and fear, he used the bee in his hands as an example. Charlie explained that he was holding a male bee, a drone, and that they did not have the ability to sting. Only females bees have stingers, and yet many of us flinch away from every bee we encounter. With that, I took the bee into my hands. Part of my brain kept telling me to be afraid. I waited for the burning sting to come, but as time passed so did the fear. It was a bit transformational to be honest.

My whole demeanor changed in that lively garden. The loud hum of buzzing around me no longer felt like a threat. I relaxed and focused on really hearing what Charlie had to say, just as hundreds of other visitors to his hives have over the years.

Charlie is a great example of a geek Missionary because his efforts focus on more than just simple awareness. He invests time in involving others in creating a solution. He exposes, educates, and encourages people to understand these issues on a deeper level. Charlie says, "I think, how do I take a person and make them a *beeliever?* Then, take that beeliever and give them enough information to become a *beeciple*, eventually turning them into *beevangelists*. If we can do that, we can *bee the change*."

I know, it is a lot of bee puns. I kind of dig it though. Puns aside, Charlie is a geek who understands t-shirt members and social media supporters are not enough. He knows that patient, dedicated effort spent engaging each person on an individual level is the slow and steady path needed to build a sustainable community.

Charlie could have focused on profit and sold out years ago, but he cared too deeply about the larger purpose. He did not want thousands of people simply buying a box for bees without the knowledge and understanding to truly help drive change.

Instead Charlie teaches classes, speaks to groups, and every day seeks out opportunities to expose someone new to the superorganism that captured his heart. He literally, and figuratively, passes along his love of bees to almost everyone he meets.

TRELLIS GEEKS

A friend of mine works as a pastor in a church. He once described to me the two kinds of work one can perform in an organization using a metaphor about how grapes are grown in a vineyard. You can do vine work or trellis work. Grape vines love to climb, so to earn the best yield growers build trellis structures to provide a path for expansion, as well as support for the fruit to later develop. To succeed over time, a viticulturist needs to invest in nurturing the vine, as well as extending and strengthening the trellis.

Vine work can best be described as the core purpose of the organization. In a church, ministering and teaching are core purposes. In a company, a core purpose is delivery of a quality product or service. *Trellis work* describes the support and infrastructure efforts required for any organization to be able to do that core work. For example, in a corporation the ability to execute core functions is enabled and expanded by trellis work like graphic design, project management, and professional development.

A special subset of geeks is engaged in the mundane and sometimes thankless trellis work of keeping communities healthy and active. Trellis geeks have no desire to be out in the front leading the show. Instead, they are the stagehands behind the curtain, silently running the show without being seen. Think the Oompa-Loompas in Willy Wonka's Chocolate Factory, but with fewer musical numbers.

Trellis-focused geeks deal with the less exciting details, such as a conference attendee wanting to know why Mountain Dew is not available in the ballroom, or printing name tags for every registrant of a 200-person *Settlers of Cataan* tourney.

The rest of us, the vine geeks, do not always pause to recognize the benefits we enjoy and the growth we experience are due in large part to the hard work of organizers, volunteers, and leaders behind the scenes. Why do geeks choose trellis work? Because it enables them to share their passions and help further a cause. In addition, many trellis geeks desire to make everyone feel welcomed and included.

In the winter of 2018 I met John, an organizer of the regional gathering of LARP gamers in Milwaukee known as *Blood & Ice*. In addition to volunteering to build this large, annual event, John also leads a local game with over 50 members. He told me, "We run this event because we did not want anyone to feel left behind."

John's primary motive is inclusion. He has a keen desire to share the love of gaming that has brought so much joy in his life. He is striving to create a safe community for anyone interested in checking it out.

He and his team work long hours each year to produce a great experience that is accessible for any player, regardless of budget, background, or experience level. He told us stories of geeks who felt bullied or ostracized by more experienced players, or those who were priced out of participation by planning groups who made the game events more about the money than the community.

John himself was treated dismissively by established players at one of the first game events he attended. He has made that memory a touchstone to ensure that sort of experience does not happen for his players. His group of gamers includes 30-something professionals with advanced degrees, broke college kids packing it in five to a hotel room, and several players with varying degrees of intellectual or emotional disability. This diverse mix of humans requires additional effort to manage and support, but as John puts it, "Everyone deserves to have fun."

Trellis workers exist in every organization. Don't forget to say thanks. We need these special geeks. Without them our passions would not have room to grow.

GEEKY INFLUENCERS

Social media is one of the most important catalysts for the recent explosion of geek culture. Suddenly, individuals have been given the opportunity to make deep passions public on a scale unheard of before. During our research, we encountered a superfan of the aforementioned *Vampire* LARP. The Gentleman Gamer, as he is known online, is a creator of dozens of informational and instructional videos designed to make exploring the game easier. He already has a following of over 16,000 viewers and has eclipsed 2 million video views.

Prior to the advent of platforms like Instagram and YouTube, a geek like this would have only had access to a small, local audience. With this new and ever-changing set of internet tools, geeky ideas and interests can spread faster than a zombie outbreak in a crowded city.

One way that geeks increase the visibility and public awareness of what they love is by producing and sharing content that explores their CoG. A fan fiction site like *Ad Astra* is a great example of an unpaid community of geeks churning out content to expand the *Star Trek* brand.

Frequently, the path of significant brand growth begins with a core group of fans communing online, only to be noticed by others on a public forum. A following needs followers, and those followers are frequently acquired on accident rather than with intent when an interesting passion goes viral for one reason or another.

Legend has it that Bronies, those who geek out on the show *"My Little Pony: Friendship is Magic,"* exploded on the scene after a small group of guys started discussion threads on social news sites like 4chan and Reddit. The group used these platforms to explore its own enthusiasm, comparing notes on the show and the personalities of favorite ponies. Other users noted the group's interactions on these sites and proceeded to ridicule the posts; Trolling is a cultural imperative on Reddit.

One day, something as magical as friendship itself happened. As one fan put it, "We were going to make fun of it, but instead everybody got hooked. And then the first pony threads exploded."

Explode, it did. The show has become wildly popular, with fan sites multiplying faster than *Tribbles in a shuttle bay*. Recently, a group of geeks published what they call the "State of the Herd Report," which uses fairly robust statistical analysis to estimate the U.S. Brony population at somewhere between 7 and 12 million people. The Brony community has inspired books, several documentaries, dozens of conventions, charity organizations like *Bronies for Good*, and more than one psychological study.

The Brony craze is another example of a red-hot trend spreading virally throughout society. The genesis of so many similar trends in recent years has followed the same model: a small group of hyper-passionate fans serve as thought leaders, expanding the brand virally through a cycle of exponential growth. The key takeaway here is that in order to create a viral phenomenon, a core of excited fans is needed: geeks.

Geeks, by virtue of their passion and willingness to invest time and energy, are influencers. Across the vast and diverse Geekosystem, they demonstrate an ability to bring people together at conferences, on social media, and in spirit.

Paul Gillin describes this effect in his book, *The New Influencers*. He says that influencers "are knowledgeable, passionate and eager to influence the markets they care about. They can be, in effect, a global online focus group that works for free. All you need to do is listen to them." Geeks energize and spread the brand without requiring the services of a pricey marketing firm or social media guru.

Influencers are "likely to understand your market, your product and your customers better than you, probably better than most of the people who work at your company." The influence of knowledgeable and passionate geeks extends to every social media platform. YouTube hosts a slew of geeks willing to talk about any and every subject audiences wish to see. If geeks like your company they will do the marketing for you.

Examples of social media influencers are everywhere. We interviewed Natalie, a makeup and fashion expert who has developed a following of thousands on Instagram. Natalie shared just how easy it is to use social platforms to send your ideas out into the world. She was quick to clarify real influence requires sticking to what you love.

Traditional marketing emphasized the need to control the message and manage the brand. This mindset of marketing is fading, but one can still empathize with nervous executives afraid to hand over the reins of their brand message to randoms online. After all, what if consumers do not like your product?

Since geeks have the power to decide what items they will promote, they also have the power to drive the market. In fact "10 percent of Americans determine what the other 90 percent buy" according to GIllin's book.

How easily can we influence the influential? A company will pay big money for a YouTuber to feature its product in a make-up tutorial or an Instagram star to promote its brand of smoothies. It is clear, even though businesses are paying influencers to advertise products, the geeks are the ones who are really in control.

Across industries, geeks are driving trends and engaging customers because they deeply understand the product and the community.

How can we curb the anxiety we feel around giving geeks a measure of control over our brand? You may not have the choice frankly. These geeks are your customers! You cannot keep the product out of their hands. Once geeks have it you cannot keep them from talking, tweeting, and vlogging about it. Instead of trying to stop them, utilize geek Missionary skills by finding, following, and rewarding them. Listening and taking the advice of these valuable consumers will allow you to build a better product on the basis of comments and complaints.

Use the Force

How can you find and engage geeks to build your community?

Organizations in every sector and industry want to recruit great people. Big money and time are spent on talent acquisition, an average of almost $4,000 per new hire. Even with huge investments, organizations bemoan the lack of quality candidates and skill gaps.

Companies also want to develop communities of customers and influencers and they invest a lot to make it happen, spending roughly $200 billion on advertising in the U.S. alone. Those same companies employ marketing firms to spend billions more. After all that money is spent these companies sometimes question their return on investment and whether the right people are being engaged. Many organizations are ignoring a powerful and low-cost resource for building brand communities: geeky influencers in their customer and employee base.

Geeks are not the panacea for your marketing woes, but they do offer the potential for incredible opportunities. Fueled by their Center of Gravity, geeks will recruit, connect, and proselytize your brand. Your task becomes empowering and equipping them to help you spread your brand message and build your community. Let's get started:

1.) Recruiting

Geeks like to share passions and recruit new followers, so let them. Instead of simply looking to human resource departments and search firms to dig up talent, have you considered empowering your most passionate geeks to connect you with candidates? If you can resist the urge to say, "That's outside the scope of their job!" for one moment, this is a smaller ask than it may first appear.

Start by talking to the most engaged among your staff, the ones who really geek out on what your company does. Ask these employees what they tell people when they talk about their job. I sometimes ask our college interns, "What do you tell your friends on campus about your job and our company?" Adding this extra step helps you learn what people are *actually* excited about, and you might be surprised.

Next, give employees permission to take initiative. Most employees never think of themselves as recruiters. Help them shift their mindset by training them how to engage if they meet someone who with an interest in their work. Do not force employees to recruit, but make it clear they are welcome and even encouraged to do so.

Finally, genuinely consider the referrals your employees bring your way. If one of your most engaged sees potential in a candidate, the person is likely worth a closer look. The respect you show toward a prospect will encourage employees to keep up their efforts.

2.) Connecting

If we are being honest, most organizations and individuals stink at using social media. We do not post often enough, we do not respond quickly enough, we do not know what is cool to post, and we hardly ever go viral. I get it. It feels like a lot of work and can be hard to understand. In my experience, companies approach the challenge of social media in three ways:

1. *Ignore social media.* The organization stands aloof while losing market share to a three-person startup with a cool app and a massive Instagram following.

2. *Find an intern.* The organization gives a college student full ownership of all social media accounts and cringes when they accidentally post pics from their weekend adventures with a wacky hashtag.

3. *Hire a specialty firm.* The organization pays through the nose for experts to take over the brand, constantly wondering what the benefits of the firm's work truly are.

Before reaching out to social media experts who may not fully understand your business, I would encourage you to take some advice from Simon Sinek, author of *Start with Why*. He argues that those who truly understand the core purpose of the organization, why it exists, can more easily explain *what* product or service is being sold and *how* it is sold.

Here is one somewhat radical idea. Try handing the keys to your company's social brand over to the geeks of the organization, even if those employees are not Twitter ninjas. Geeks do not feel hampered by most of the significant barriers impeding a successful social media presence because they understand what customers want right now, which is more likely to go viral. And, of course, geeks will not forget to post because they have a lot to say on the subject. Not to mention, these employees will also be using the expert perspectives your geeky customers crave.

The technical skills needed to operate social media platforms can be taught or outsourced, but the content, the passion, and the attention rarely can. It could be risky to ask your geekiest product engineer to run your customer message board, but maybe not as risky as the alternatives.

3.) Proselytizing

Preach! As a small business owner I am constantly telling our company's story. I geek out on FOCUS Training. I drank the non-carbonated fruit beverage at age 17 and never looked back. After 20 years, I eagerly tell my FOCUS story to anyone who will listen. The tale has evolved into an essential tool in my recruitment efforts, team motivation, and sales approach.

I had planned on pursuing a career in marketing since high school. I found myself attending an endless run of professional development workshops, hoping to capture some sort of magical career-launching secret from the professionals sitting on this or that leadership panel. I was so hooked I even sold coupon books and holiday wreaths just to attend.

By eleventh grade I had been through enough of these conferences I could write the textbook on them. In the back conference room of some downtown hotel a corporate marketing manager would spend a day name dropping well-known clients in an effort to make his job sound cool.

With minimal eye contact, this speaker would breeze over the hard work required for the job, namely the extensive research and math skills needed. His company-approved presentation deck would either contain content so simple it was painful to hear, or the jargon and industry speak would be so intense we would have no idea what was being said. It was pretty brutal for a high school student.

At a conference in Milwaukee in 1997, I walked into a meeting room and was surprised to find myself swept up in something new. It was an engaging, high-energy learning experience. We worked in teams, sharing our ideas and setting personal goals to use what we had learned. It was actually fun! I was enthralled by the speaker, Melissa, and her company's approach. I had to learn this magic.

Who were these people? I looked back at my conference program and memorized the name FOCUS Training.

Two years later I was heading off to college in Madison. I had kept FOCUS close, attending every one of its conferences I could, even landing a student leadership position that secured Melissa as my mentor. I knew that she and her business partner, Todd, had plans to open a new headquarters in Milwaukee that summer.

It felt like my best chance, so I asked point-blank for a job. "Sure," Melissa replied, "but we can't pay you."

All I heard was the yes.

I packed my bags, took a job waiting tables, found a roommate, and worked full-time in our little startup for four summers while I finished my degree. I loved the feeling of building something new, the thrill of being on stage, and the culture of passion and shared ownership. I just knew that these were my people and this was my place.

The story continues for 20 years, but not much has changed since that first moment I felt inspired at a leadership conference. I still geek on the work and the family we assembled. I love that I can tell people FOCUS was my first real job and it is my retirement plan.

Your organization almost certainly has found its roots in a similar story: The legend of a founder working long nights to build the business in a garage or dorm room or the story of the CEO starting as an intern. My partners have great stories, too. So do many of our long-serving team members. These personal stories define our brand, a lesson we did not always understand. We tried too hard to control the message. This is a mistake that many leaders in many businesses have made or are still making.

Years ago our leadership team discussed teaching all our employees a common elevator pitch. What should every FOCUS team member say when asked about the firm? To help us build our business we needed more than just our three partners sharing the brand with the world. We had to give up control, a tough step for any entrepreneur. Hard as it may be, we needed to do it. We recognized we were not the only people who understood what made our products and organization great.

We worried about consistency and professionalism. Brand clarity, integrity, fidelity, and a slew of other terms were bandied about as we flexed our rich corporate-speak vocabulary. In the midst of this heady work on our brand message, it became clear that even we did not agree on what our brand really was.

Together we brainstormed about our organization's value proposition: custom-built training experiences, genuine facilitators, and experiential methods. However, it was clear that beyond these shared organizational capabilities the brand perspectives we each held were as diverse as the members of our team.

We each had our own story woven into the fabric of the company. So we decided to encourage each one of our geeky team members to tell the story of FOCUS from their own perspective instead of from one manufactured statement. The result? A team full of people who talks about our company like owners would, not just in painstakingly specific terms, but with genuine passion.

Ask your organization and yourself the following questions:

- Do you hold too tightly to control of your brand?

- Are you forcing a manufactured brand message when an organic approach could be more genuine?

- What can you do to relax your grip and give your team and customers more room to run?

If you hold on too tightly to your brand, you stand in the way of the geeks who want to pour their love into it. So, stop sending cease-and-desist letters to the college kids breaking apart your product on their YouTube channel. Instead, blow these students' minds when you invite yourself onto their show, bringing along a secret prototype yet to be released.

Let your employees write their own social media posts rather than just pasting in the generic copy and stock photos from your corporate marketing team. Sure, there is some risk to mitigate, but consider the opportunity cost of all this control? Engagement, energy, and passion are a high price to pay.

If you owned an exotic sports car, would you stick to a 35 mph speed limit? Restricting yourself to a lower speed is obviously safer, but if safety was your goal why spend big money on all that horsepower?

In the same way, as a leader in an organization you leave a powerful capacity for growth on the shelf when you limit your customers and employees. Geeks want to share, which drives them to recruit, engage, connect, and evangelize. Tap into that Missionary zeal and hang onto your hat.

QUESTIONS TO CONSIDER

1. How can you engage the geeks in your organization to help you recruit talented people with similar passions?

2. What are your organization's opportunities to improve your social media presence? Are there ways that the geeks on your team or in your customer base can help give feedback or create content?

3. How are you telling your brand story today? How can you engage others who geek on your product or organization and inject more personality and passion into that story?

MEET A GEEK 6: OAK & SHIELD BAR

What do popular sitcoms like *Cheers*, *Friends*, *How I Met Your Mother*, and *Seinfeld* all have in common? Each are about 30 minutes long, each are comedies, each have relatable characters, and each has a meet up spot at a fictitious local restaurant, bar, or cafe.

The meet-up spot is a place the group of friends all go to hangout and talk through their problems, entertain one another, and meet new people. Phoebe plays "Smelly Cat" at New York's Central Perk coffee shop, Jerry and George argue about nothing and everything in their usual booth at Monk's Café, and Sam and Diane fall in and out of love at the Boston pub Cheers.

These fictitious places are where our favorite characters' lives unfold. In real life, these safe havens from work, family, and stress exist too. Geeks come together in local comic book stores, at convention halls, and other niche locales.

A geeky bar called Oak & Shield recently popped up in Milwaukee and has instantly become a hub for geeks and gamers of all kinds. The name sounds like something out of a *D&D* campaign, but when we sat down and talked to the bar's owner, she let us know the name was actually inspired by a character from *The Hobbit*, the Elven King Thorin Oakenshield.

The bar would have been named Milwaukee's Board Game Bar and Grill had her business partner gotten his way. Luckily, Lynn spoke up and voiced her opinion. She says, "I tease that he likes to give things names that describe the thing exactly and are far too long."

Lynn has experience catering to geeky clients. She previously opened two other geek-centric establishments. The concept of the Oak & Shield was conceived over coffee with the owner of the Board Game Barrister, a local game store.

Of the bar's inception, Lynn shares, "I knew I had found someone who had a very special, laser-focused view of business that would pair well with my style. We share the vision of building community through games, I just had the bonus of alcohol. It turned out that he had dreams of opening his own cafe or pub, so it was a natural fit for us to work together."

The bar was opened on May 4. Get it? May the 4th be with you? Lynn collapsed at the end of that 20-hour work day, exhausted, yet proud of the work she had accomplished. The smiles on the faces of her very first customers reassured her that this bar was needed. The successful opening taught Lynn "how much we need this, a bar to go to and drink and hang out with people who get us."

To work for this geek, you yourself must be a geek. And to work at Oak & Shield, it must first be decided whether the server is a right fit for the clientele. "We focus on hiring people with the kind of personality that others are naturally drawn to. We want our staff to facilitate the kind of community we want to be a part of. That means that your bartender is the person you go to when you want to discuss the new game you just bought, and they make suggestions on other items you're probably going to enjoy as well." Your server will not just be serving you drinks, she will also divulge pro tips for the favorite game you are playing because she plays it too.

Let me paint you a picture. You open a menu and every entrée listed is a reference to geek culture. Order a drink and you have the option of choosing from a range of craft cocktails like a Butterbeer from the wizarding world of *Harry Potter*. Head over to the game shelf and you can choose from an endless display of board games, discovering many you had never heard of before.

Your night might conclude with some of the most intense set of karaoke you can imagine. Musical theater geeks entertain the crowd with sets of songs they have performed thousands of times before on stage, in front of friends, or privately for their bathroom mirror.

Lynn's mission is simple: "We make it a priority to unite people through games, by making purposeful introductions and hosting events where people of all skill levels and backgrounds can come together and play."

Some of her favorite experiences at the bar have been events where "people [all] come together over one common goal, feeling, triumph, or event." Oak & Shield has hosted a huge *Dragon Ball Z* party, a wide assortment of cosplay nights, and is gearing up for its third annual *Harry Potter*-inspired Yule Ball.

The Yule Ball is a two-night event that takes place downtown in a large ballroom. Geeks flock to this event. It sells out out every year. Attendees are taught by instructors how to gracefully waltz with their partners, local vendors sell craft items in the appropriately titled Diagon Alley, and cosplay is in full effect as characters don luxurious suits and gowns. The community has nicknamed the event Wizard Prom. Fitting.

Lynn recognizes that not everyone geeks deep. Inevitably, people will wander into the bar who do not understand the geek community or the appeal of such a bar. Haters gonna hate. Lynn does not waste her time trying to change their minds.

She says, "I'm not going to try to convince anyone that they should geek out. I think the people who are naturally drawn to this community are the ones who find something in it that resonates with them deeply enough for them to find value in it. While I think everyone can find something here they will enjoy, sometimes I'd rather not waste the energy on those who aren't interested. I'll lead you to it, but you have to want it.

Sometimes I legitimately forget that there are muggles out there, until I have to explain to them what a convention is, or how my bar works. A lot of people on the outside think that geeks don't drink, and upon hearing that we have video games and tabletop games, they don't get how we can stay in business. So, I have to liken it to a pool hall or playing darts in bars; Connect with them on a level they will understand. It's frustrating though, especially if they want to put it down without taking the time to understand. I usually just feel sorry for them."

Lynn has seen firsthand the impact her businesses have had on the community. Her first venture into the geekosystem started with 42 Lounge. After five years of owning and operating this geeky nightclub, Lynn was met with circumstances that forced her to close it down. On the bar's final night of existence, geeks from out of state drove in to say their goodbyes to "the place where they had formed friendships and memories of a lifetime." The Lounge was much more than just a nightclub.

There are other establishments happy to sell you alcohol, food, and a place to hang out, but Lynn's club was a home for the patrons. "It's not about the thing you're eating or drinking, it's about having a home to go to where people understand you, and that's what geek bars and restaurants do. They make it okay for people who have felt ostracized their entire lives to enjoy the things that they liked in private in a public place, and share those experiences with others."

Everyone needs a hangout, a meet-up spot, a Central Perk. At Oak & Shield geeks are given the chance to socialize and let the plot lines of their life play out. The karaoke geeks entertain like Phoebe. Gamers eating a *D&D*-themed burge argue over everything and nothing like George and Jerry in Monk's Cafe. True love has blossomed at the Yule Ball as Ron and Hermione cosplayers waltz their way into the sunset, just like Sam and Diane in *Cheers*.

PART 4
CONCLUSION

MEET A GEEK 7: ROLE PLAYING GAMERS

Whether you are a gamer or not, *Dungeons & Dragons* is now something of a household name. A worldwide phenomenon, it has been estimated that since its inception in 1974 it has been played by more than thirty million people. It's founder, Gary Gygax, is somewhat of a legend in the geekosystem.

Gygax was raised in Lake Geneva, Wisconsin. Following a brief stint in the Marines, he became obsessed with playing a strategy war game called *Gettysburg*. Late nights were spent, not with his wife and young family, but in friends' basements shouting commands to his imaginary troops. His fascination with the game led to his involvement organizing a now-famous gathering, Gen Con, and the eventual development of his own fantasy game.

After a day at his office job in Chicago Gygax would commute back to Lake Geneva and spend his nights at the typewriter developing the story lines for *D&D.* He allowed himself to commit fully to his imagination, emptying the vivid story lines from his mind.

Gygax has said that to ignore his creative urges was not an option. "I write mainly because I have so much information inside I just have to. The main 'no-no' I have is not to ignore an urge to write. Ideas are ephemeral, slip away too quickly, so when the muse is there go like hell."

Seeing the enjoyment his family, friends, and community of gamers experienced while testing *D&D*, Gygax was positive the major gaming companies would be desperate to produce his game. Not one company took an interest in the idea. Determined to make his dream a reality, Gygax and his team decided to self-publish. The risk paid off and *D&D* became a huge success, until a wild period in the 80s.

A series of tragic events tarnished the brand's reputation. Parents believed the game would act as a gateway to a darker future. The game became a social taboo as *D&D* and its players found themselves at the center of mass hysteria. It was linked to murders, satanic rituals, even teen suicides. It was banned by schools, demonized by church groups, and even criminalized by some courts. Law enforcement began to report to media that a suspect "was known to play *D&D*" in the same tone reserved for mention of tortured animals or gang membership.

In reality, *D&D* was a vehicle for the introverted geek to form friendships and bond with other gamers in epic imagined adventures. In 2011, Gregory Harrison and James Van Haneghan conducted studies on gifted students of both middle school and high school age. They found that these children experienced "higher levels of insomnia, anxiety, and fear of death than their peers."

In an effort to resolve these problems, the researchers introduced fantasy games like *D&D* as a form of therapy. Creatively tackling the absurd scenarios that take place during the course of a campaign showed students how to work through their problems while still having fun. After all, if you can handle a fire-breathing red dragon or the sinister magics of a mad wizard, how scary can lunchroom politics be?

At the game table, camaraderie forms organically. "When a group of people play a game together, they enter a sort of alternate reality where friendships form at an accelerated rate. The players have limited time, so things have to move quickly, and they've got a specific goal, so they focus on winning, not on the normal rules of social interaction."

We went to our local comic book and gaming store to sit down with some RPGers and discuss the community today. Cody, that evening's *Pathfinder* Game Master, welcomed us enthusiastically and wove us into the game. He explained, "Our community is open and accepting of anyone. I see equally new and veteran players each night. As a Game Master, you are the world for the players. You are everyone they meet. You are there to be a referee and you are there to see them complete their quests and objectives to make it to the end of the game."

He confessed to us that he likes to watch stand-up comedy routines to warm up for games and prepare to entertain his players. Cody enjoys the different people he interacts with and the challenge of discovering how to persuade and navigate the fictional settings together. "The game teaches you how to talk to all kinds of people, especially those who are not friendly, and engage them."

Josh, a player at the table, says the key to recruiting new players involves selling gamers on the promise of living out a fantasy scenario they wish they could in real life. An avid attendee at conventions in the area, he mentioned to us that he enjoys going a step further and dressing up as his favorite characters.

Josh uses his geekiness to give back to his city. He is part of a group that dresses in fantasy costumes and participates in local charity events. With the help of a Milwaukee artist he created a full suit of armor. As I've mentioned, making chain mail is not for the weak of heart. Josh told us it took six months of labor and a $1,000 investment to create this suit of armor. Knighthood comes at a cost.

He also shared with us that many RPGers do not fit the stereotype of a traditional gamer. "Some people who play have super serious jobs in real life but you would never know it. Did you know that Vin Diesel plays *D&D*? Why wouldn't Vin like *D&D*? He acts in adventure movies that parallel the game pretty strongly." Food for thought.

Creative director, graphic designer, and *D&D* enthusiast Nick does not shy away from talking about games at work. He told us, "I told people in the office that I was a gamer and now we are always talking about it; It's my hobby."

Although the group wrote a six-hour campaign together and travels to Gen Con every year, of his gamer friends Nick wants to be clear: "We aren't just dressed as wizards." Time spent at the gaming table is about more than fantasy. The group enjoys each other's company and finds the time spent relaxing.

Nick could not have been more excited to share about his time at Gen Con, "The role-playing renaissance has exploded!" This convention is the Mecca of gaming, with over 72,000 gamers gathering together in Indianapolis every August to geek out together.

Conventions offer geeks a venue to share in their culture without fear of judgment. A strong sense of community is formed among attendees. A building full of gamers who understands your passion is waiting just for you. Nick explains, "I love being around others who understand geek culture. I have never been to a convention where there was an issue or a dispute. No one is mean to each other there."

Nick was not always so outspoken about his passions. Growing up with three athletic brothers, he felt like an outcast when he stayed inside to read game books and design maps.

Nick was quick to recognize the same skills that make his campaigns so successful are the very skills he uses to excel at work. As a creative director he is in the business of selling ideas, problem solving, and managing people. Nick utilizes his storytelling skills every time he shares his latest design proposal with a client.

He also uses his graphic design skills to help create games with Milwaukee-based company Minion Games. Nick ran into the owner at a game store and the two connected instantly. Minion had many ideas for future games but needed an artist to help create the tangible product. Together they have created two projects. Nick shared a tip for game designers that he learned along the way, "When you design a game, you start by cutting cardboard boxes to figure out the game's mechanics. You create the artistic design last."

Gamers like Nick are the creators of some of our favorite video games, television shows, and board games. Ian Bogost, professor of media studies and interactive computing at the Georgia Institute of Technology, identifies the RPG players of the 70s and 80s as those same geeks who utilized the microcomputer to give us groundbreaking entertainment. "In the same way that Tolkien's fantasy fiction inspired the first role-playing games, *D&D* provided a model for the first video games."

Gamers come in all shapes and sizes. The passion for fantasy-fueled nights transforms in the light of day to an unwavering energy channeled toward work, charities, entertainment, and the environment.

GEEK DEEP

Throughout this book we explored the abilities that are unlocked when individuals understand and embrace their Center of Gravity. We have seen geeks mastering complex skills because they are invested in an activity deeply enough to push past boredom and other plateaus of progress. We met geeks who created innovative solutions to challenging real-life problems by tapping into their geek skills and interests. We observed geeks building communities and spreading important messages through the power of their passions.

With so many examples of geeky superpowers in action, one could be tempted to think these stories are more common than not, that these intriguing characters and their stories are now mainstream and accepted. To an extent, this is true. The boundaries of the mainstream have shifted. Behaviors and interests that used to place you on the fringe have become more commonplace. But, we have a long way to go if we want to truly activate the great geeky potential of people in our teams and communities.

You can arrive on opening night for the midnight showing of the latest movie in your favorite sci-fi franchise and very few eyebrows will be raised. That feels like progress. But try posting selfies from the line dressed in dark robes and Darth Maul makeup, while choreographing a battle with your movie-quality replica double-bladed saber. I think you know what kind of looks are coming your way. There is a line, beyond which you start to think about limiting the scope of people with whom you share these moments because they won't understand. They will judge.

Even in a world where our greater connectivity and shifting cultural norms have liberalized much of what we once found geeky, there is a deeply rooted hypocrisy in how our society views passion and the passionate. I believe the basic challenge we face is not the need to keep moving the line, but that the line itself has become warped or misinterpreted.

The idea of the mainstream evolved out of an important element of all successful societies: shared behavioral norms. To coexist in any community we agree, explicitly and implicitly, to certain codes of normative behavior that are meant to keep us safe. I don't walk into your house uninvited. You don't help yourself to my cup of coffee. These can be codified into laws or simply enforced by social pressure.

Norms build culture and culture has momentum. It reinforces itself through stories and social modeling. It is expanded and shaped by the leaders we choose to follow and the events we give significance. The result in many societies is that our behavioral norms have shifted purpose. Rather than simple agreements to keep us safe, norms driven by the momentum of our culture take on new levels of expectation to make us feel comfortable. Comfort and safety are not equivalent, but are easy to conflate when left unexamined.

The line here is murky. Psychological safety is still safety, but there is a difference between "this behavior hurts me emotionally or mentally" and "this behavior is difficult for me to understand or empathize with, and as such makes me uncomfortable". Perhaps because this line is so difficult to define, particularly in a collective way, our social norms have a tendency to become more and more restrictive. As comfort norms layer onto our cultural expectations we see the zone of acceptable behaviors narrow. A mainstream is born, with all the limitations and shackles on our potential that have been discussed throughout this book.

To me, one of the most interesting examples of this cultural effect is the Satanic Panic of the 1980s, specifically in relation to *Dungeons & Dragons* and similar role-playing games. Starting as early as 1979 with the disappearance of James Dallas Egbert III in the steam tunnels of Michigan State University, these storytelling games were tied in the media to unfortunate events like suicides and murders. The games and the subculture of gamers was poorly understood by mainstream society, and in the absence of good information assumptions and speculation ran wild.

Self-proclaimed anti-occult campaigners like Patricia Pulling, founder of Bothered About Dungeons & Dragons (BADD), responded to terrible events like the depression-driven suicide of her son with aggressive action in the courts and media. They blamed the games' fictional themes of magic and non-Christian religions for inspiration, subliminal suggestion, or even demonic possession.

The media reacted to this burst of interest with great enthusiasm and an unfortunate dearth of researched fact. Books were written, fictionally amplifying the real stories for dramatic effect. Made-for-TV movies were produced with big name stars like Tom Hanks. Even *60 Minutes* lent credibility to the craze in 1985 when it aired a special on the subject. In this show they gave air time to Pulling and other critics alongside Gary Gygax and the team at TSR, creators of Dungeons & Dragons.

All this hysteria started from a kernel of discomfort and misunderstanding. These role playing games were relatively new and unknown. They were outside of the cultural norm. Mainstream society reacted from a place of fear rather than fact. Institutions of culture then reinforced a false narrative with stories and legends.

This has happened countless times in human history. Discomfort with the cultural practices of displaced Roma people in Europe evolved into derogatory "gypsy" mythology, casting them as criminals, witches, and child traffickers. In the late 1990s unease with the rising integration of technology into our daily life helped drive overblown anxiety that the Y2K computer bug would destroy the world economy and bring on a global stone age. Humans do not have a great track record of avoiding this slippery slope towards fearful rejection of something new and different.

There are many more examples of social norms run amok, racing past their original purpose of keeping communities safe through the prevention of risky behavior. As culture expands the mainstream we see behavioral norms extended to include not just what keeps us safe, but what keeps us comfortable. Things we do not yet understand, are not accustomed to, that don't align to our personal value system, all take on an air of danger. When they bump up against the mainstream we label them weird, foreign, or fringe.

Wild overreactions can lead to terrifying consequences like people bankrupting themselves in a panic or the targeting and abuse of ethnic groups. But these outcomes can also activate the mainstream in counterpoint, when the larger culture awakens to the dangers of the reactive behavior. Though it may take a heartbreakingly long time, eventually we acknowledge that it ought to be unacceptable to bully a kid with a speech impediment or deny affordable housing to people from a certain part of the world. Moderating these extremes, though important, is not the true goal of this book.

There is a more subtle and widespread price paid by society. Think about the potential that can be unlocked when a person becomes free of the social risks attached to pursuing their Center of Gravity. We talked about this potential throughout the book; mastering complex skills, innovating to create powerful new ideas, building strong communities, and more. Now, think about how many millions of people will never come close to that level of engagement. Think about that untapped promise lying dormant in our world.

So what can individuals, leaders, and organizations do to push back? Is it possible? What I am describing is a tectonic cultural shift, but each of us can contribute. It starts by working on how you engage with these cultural norms, your own CoG, and the passions of those around you.

CLOSET GEEKS

Some of us know our Center of Gravity and even explore it, but do so quietly within a small community of peers. These closet geeks will sneak off to the convention in San Diego but tell everyone at work they are on a golf trip. They live a second life on the web, connecting to people they may never meet in person. I was that closet geek in high school, playing *Magic the Gathering* after school in a little used section of the cafeteria out of sight of any random passerby that might judge me.

Closet geeks have access to some of the superpowers. They know their CoG and embrace it, so the abilities of the Master and Maker are not out of reach. It is their fear of exposure that denies them the benefits of an active role in community that Missionary geeks enjoy. For closet geeks, the next step is intimidating. You have to share the love and let your geek flag fly!

I remember the first time I asked a group of college friends if they had ever played *D&D*. I had not played in years and had a hankering to run a game. This felt like quite a risk. I had established a reputation in the group and finally felt accepted. Plus, you know, there were girls in the room.

I took a deep breath and asked, making sure to use a tone that would allow me to act like I had been joking if utterly rejected. Instead, the reaction was somewhere north of the worst-case scenario. Nobody in the group had played but one guy said he had always wanted to try. Two girls said it sounded weird but they did not really know anything about it so they did not want to judge. Everyone else said if there was beer involved, they would try just about anything. And so I pushed forward.

This is not the story of how I boldly unveiled my geekiness and magically converted a room full of people into hardcore RPG players. I offered to host a game. People showed up. Some just watched. Lots of questions were asked. Some seemed to have fun. Some said they didn't understand the appeal. At the end of the night one girl turned to the group as she headed for the door and said, "I wasn't sure about this, but I had fun. When are we going to play again? Can I be a wizard next time? That seems cooler." This is what victory looks like.

I think many closet geeks hold back out of fear of the worst case. No one likes being rejected for their interests. To you I say, if you have critics it means you are doing something worth talking about. Most likely the harsh reaction you fear will not be the actual outcome. Your mind is exaggerating the likelihood of the worst-case scenario because the future is unknown and ambiguous. It is working in the absence of good information, allowing assumptions and speculation to run wild. Sound familiar? We are good at creating terrifying monsters in the dark, when most of the dangers out there are just tripping hazards.

Others hesitate because their expectations are too high, thinking what if the world does not love this like I love this? Frankly, they probably won't. In my experience, the reality tends to fall somewhere in the middle. Some people just will not get it. Some will. A rare few will fall madly in love and bug you every night that week about getting in another game.

It is a bit like dating. Some first dates will be a bust. Some will lead to a second date or even a relationship. And, from time to time a quick drink after work leads to a lifelong partnership. You will never know the outcome if you don't take the leap. Many find it is worth the risk.

You can taste a wine alone and have a powerful experience. Without a companion or community though, you won't get to describe the bouquet of that Napa Cabernet to someone who can contrast their own experience. You won't get to debate whether that is a blackberry or huckleberry note you detect. You won't get to fondly compare it to the intense Bordeaux you shared at a family dinner party in 2014. Geeking out alone will just never be as fulfilling as geeking out with your squad.

SEARCH FOR CENTER

The greater challenge is waiting for the non-geeks out there. What should you do if you have simply not discovered or embraced your Center of Gravity? Are you the self-labeled boring one, who has yet to really get excited about an interest. Are you intensely curious about something, but have yet to look closer out of fear of how it would be perceived by the mainstream?

If you have not found a CoG you can unlock the enthusiasm and energy of geeking out on something. Explore strange new interests, seek out new experiences, and boldly go where you have not gone before! This can be scary. I will just offer two pieces of advice. Call them rules for first contact.

In any science fiction story involving first contact with an alien species, there is a lot of tension. Sometimes the aliens land on our planet and descend a ramp in a cloud of mist. Other stories place humans in the role of new arrivals. We introduce ourselves to a society and try to put our best foot forward. In either case, the risks seem colossal. A misunderstanding or a cultural faux pas could lead to disaster.

Our fictional future selves establish rules for first contact for that reason. They define guidelines and best practices to minimize the risk and encourage a positive beginning to the relationship. The Prime Directive, containment protocols, and highly trained contact teams are all examples of how humans in science fiction handle meeting alien life.

If you don't know your own CoG yet, work on your rules for first contact. You want to be ready for either scenario. Will something interesting land in your back yard? Will you go out looking for it on another world? Either way, your mindset will play a critical role in your success.

Train your mind to react to facts rather than from fear. We naturally resist the different and the new which is how our amygdala attempts to keep us safe. When we roamed the wilderness in small nomadic tribes approaching an unknown animal or stranger could mean great danger. Our innate distrust of the unknown is an evolutionary byproduct, but this reaction is outdated in our modern lives.

If you are still searching for your passion, can you really afford to reject new experiences? To find a Center of Gravity requires you to seek out opportunities with boldness and intention. Open the mind to possibilities, such as the idea that you might actually have fun at a stamp collector's convention or coding an app.

When we quickly reject new experiences we greatly limit our chances of feeling the driving passion of geeks. Many of us have that single friend who wants to find a romantic partner, but refuses to go out, does not like meeting new people, and walks into first dates looking for reasons to say no. Every time we hear that person complain about their situation we think, "Well what are you doing about it?" Do not incorporate these practices into your own life as you look for a passion to pursue.

Online dating tools like Match.com have been wildly successful because they expand the pool of potential candidates, dramatically increasing your odds of finding a compatible partner. The same idea applies to geeking out. The more opportunities you open yourself up to the better the chances of you finding a CoG match.

Consider a proactive approach of seeking out new things to try in the hopes of falling into your CoG. When exploring the galaxy a smart starship captain starts by investigating their own star system. In other words, there is no need to immediately leap into the most extreme or random pursuits. Begin your search for something you love with things adjacent to what you already like. If you like watching wrestling shows, maybe you could find a video channel about how new wrestlers create their character. Or maybe you could visit a local wrestling gym to watch some amateur matches. Meet some people with similar interests and tag along to see what else they enjoy.

As you explore, do so with open eyes and an open mind. Your amygdala is primed to react to the newness around you as unknown and risky. Push through the natural reaction of fear by asking questions. What? How? Why? As the information flows in, your frontal cortex will reassert itself and you can shape your opinions of this potential CoG based on the facts.

This is your best rule for first contact: *curiosity over cynicism*. When you attend your first event of miniature electric train enthusiasts, fight back against your gut-level reaction to judge these folks for the hundreds of hours they spent building a scale model of the old west town of Deadwood. Instead, ask them how they did it! Find out what is it about this that interests them and how they discovered it. What else are they into that makes them feel like this? You are on a hunt for the same magic of brain chemistry, so be vigilant for the subtle temptation to revert to a judgmental mindset.

The same rule works when you are in passive search mode, watching as the flying saucer lands in your town. In real life, this looks like a friend inviting you to check out their cousin's punk band or offering to loan you their box set of *Doctor Who* DVDs. Remember that Missionary geeks are eager to share. Take advantage of that enthusiasm by listening with the right mindset to help you discover potential new interests.

I have spent dozens of hours reading Dr. Seuss's *Green Eggs and Ham* to my sons. That Sam-I-Am character seems like a classic geek recruiter to me. Sam is persistent and excited, eager to bring a new member into his culinary club. The lesson of the book is just as useful for adults searching for a purpose and passion as it is for five-year-olds learning to eat their veggies.

As you continue the search for your own Center of Gravity, be open-minded to the enthusiastic pitch geeks make. Since you have not yet found your community, you should seriously consider taking the geek up on their offer. While not every community in the Geekosystem will be right for you, you cannot afford to discount a group out-of-hand before experiencing what it has to offer.

Next time your coworker invites you to check out the community theater production they are headed to after work, give it a try before you take a hard pass. You say you do not like one-act plays? Try them. Try them and you may, I say.

Do not despair! If you have made it this far into the book and still feel like you are reading about other people, let us acknowledge something very important right here and right now. **You are a geek!** We all are. You may not know the 43,252,003,274,489,856,000 possible combinations on a Rubik's cube, or how *Pokémon's Charmeleon* evolves into *Charizard*, but you geek out on something.

Not convinced? At every conference or training program where I speak about geeks, I encounter people who have a difficult time connecting with the idea of being a geek. They say, "I'm not into that sci-fi stuff." Ironically, the Geekosystem also has some of its own mainstream tropes. The idea that certain things are geeky and others are cool is misleading cool people like you! Do not let yourself get hung up on the stereotypes. Your inner geek may be less obvious than a Trekkie's, but I can assure you that it is there.

We all love something. The key difference between geeks and everyone else is that geeks are honest with the world and with themselves about their Center of Gravity. They have accepted and embraced the truth. Now it is your turn. What is your guilty pleasure? What are you hooked on? What do you invest more time on than most people?

Maybe you are a fantasy football geek, pouring hours into preparing for your draft each season. Maybe you geek on reality television, investing more time in the drama of a group of housewives than you would like to admit. Is it knitting? Sudoku? Discovering hole-in-the-wall restaurants? Climbing mountains? Table tennis? Black-and-white classic cinema? Are you a history geek? A wrestling geek? An antiques geek?

Maybe you geek on your kids or grandkids, regaling everyone you meet with adorable stories and a sampling of the 12,000 photos you have stored in your phone. Or maybe you are a pet parent, doing the exact same thing with images of your fur babies. Look in the mirror and broaden your idea of what geeking out looks like. Your geek potential is just waiting to be recognized. The first step is admitting it.

Yes, you are a geek. Transparency and self-awareness are freeing and empowering. Geeks dig deeper than the mainstream deems appropriate. Geeks are unafraid to embrace what they love, which removes the shackles social norms would otherwise impose on the spirit.

You can do this. Embrace your CoG or go looking for it. Open your mind, explore your interests, and share your passion with the world around you. Join a community or build one.

This is how we repair the mainstream. This is how we realign our social norms and free up the untapped wellspring of potential. We do it one geek at a time, starting with you. You cannot do it for someone else. You cannot legislate it or force it on an organization or team. You can only model the mindset and support it in others.

Every person who goes geek in the way we've discussed nudges the flywheel of culture further in the direction of support and inclusion. It will take a lot of us to shift the momentum, but the Geekosystem is vast and more are joining up every day. I believe that geeking out is contagious, a benevolent epidemic. It is like if the zombie apocalypse arrived but getting infected meant you transformed into a happier, more productive version of yourself surrounded by a community of people who understand and accept you. In that world I think most of us would not run away. We would stand and say, "Bite me".

Join us. *Resistance is futile.*

GEEK
GLOSSARY

Battlestar Galactica

MATT SAYS:

"I never watched the original series. The SciFi channel reboot, however, was life-changing. It still stands out in my mind as some of the greatest television storytelling ever produced. *Make the time*."

QUICK SUMMARY:

A science fiction media franchise created by Glen A. Larson. The story takes place after the destruction of the Twelve Colonies of Mankind, with survivors fleeing on gigantic battleship and spacecraft carrier Battlestar Galactica, led by Commander Adama, in search of a fabled thirteenth colony, planet Earth.

The franchise began in 1978, followed by a short-run sequel series known as *Galactica 1980*. The series has inspired book adaptations, novels, comic books, a board game, and video games. In 2003, a two-part, three-hour miniseries was produced, which led to a weekly television series running until 2009. Prequel series *Caprica* aired in 2010.

Brony

MATT SAYS:

"These guys are some of my favorite geeks. It takes a lot of guts to tell people you are a 35 year old man whose favorite pony is Rainbow Dash because she reminds you to take risks. There may be no better example of the power of our Center of Gravity to build supportive communities."

QUICK SUMMARY:

A fan of *My Little Pony: Friendship is Magic* who falls outside the target demographic, namely male teenagers and young adults. See the Missionaries chapter for more information. Begin your search: *https://poniverse.net/*.

Charizard

MATT SAYS:

"He's no Jigglypuff."

QUICK SUMMARY:

A well-loved *Pokémon* created to resonate with North American audiences because of their preference for strong and powerful characters. Charizard's pre-evolutions, Charmander and Charmeleon, are ground-bound lizard-like creatures, but Charizard resembles a large, traditional flying European dragon.

Charlie Parker

MATT SAYS:

"Charlie Parker's story is the template for every great *VH1: Behind the Music* episode ever, a shooting star whose obsessive talent burned him out before his time."

QUICK SUMMARY:

Also known as yardbird, or bird for short, Charlie Parker was an American jazz saxophonist and composer active from the 1930s to the 1950s. Parker was a highly influential jazz soloist and a leading figure in the development of bebop, a form of jazz characterized by fast tempos, virtuosic technique, and advanced harmonies. In 1974, his recordings were inducted into the Grammy Hall of Fame.

Doctor Who

MATT SAYS:

"If there was a food chain for geeks, Whovians (those who geek upon the 'Good Doctor'), would be apex predators: Amazing *and* terrifying."

QUICK SUMMARY:

A British science fiction television series produced by the BBC. Original production of *Doctor Who* took place from 1963 to 1989. The story follows the adventures of a Time Lord known as "the Doctor," an extraterrestrial being from planet Gallifrey. The Doctor explores the universe in time-traveling spaceship TARDIS, its exterior a blue British police box.

The show has become a part of British pop culture, with numerous spin-offs, including comic books, films, novels, audio dramas, and a television series. After the original lead Doctor became ill, regeneration was introduced to the plotline to allow other actors to take over the role.

Twelve actors have played the Doctor over the years. The story explains the introduction of new actors as a Time Lord trait of the Doctor to take on a new body and personality as a way to recover from severe injury.

Dragon Ball Z

MATT SAYS:

"My favorite part of *DBZ* was also the most frustrating. Every fight scene would be sooooooo very long. This show built tension the same way that medieval Christians built cathedrals, so slowly you might die before the end. I guess they thought if it took three episodes to build up the power in a single Goku punch that would be *some* punch. I guess they were right."

QUICK SUMMARY:

A Japanese anime television series following the adventures of protagonist martial artist Goku who, along with his companions, defends the Earth against an assortment of villains ranging from intergalactic space fighters and conquerors, unnaturally powerful androids, and nearly indestructible creatures.

The series ran from 1988-1995. While the original *Dragon Ball* anime followed Goku from his childhood into adulthood, *Dragon Ball Z* is a continuation of his adult life that parallels the maturation of his sons, Gohan and Goten, as well as the evolution of his rivals, Piccolo and Vegeta, from enemies into allies.

The series has been dubbed in the U.S., Australia, Europe, India, and Latin America.

Dungeons & Dragons

MATT SAYS:

"Over the years I have invited many people to play *D&D* with me and have been rejected again and again. Let me encourage you to *just try it!* Once you push past the stigma of dorky shut-ins swilling soda in their parents' basement, I promise you will be pleasantly surprised.

Like most games, this one can be intimidating until you understand the rules and is much more fun when played with people you enjoy being around. It is also one of the more challenging games ever created because your options are nearly unlimited. If you are still unsure, play your first night with a couple bottles of wine at the table; It helps."

QUICK SUMMARY:

A fantasy tabletop role-playing game designed by Gary Gygax and Dave Arneson in 1974. The game was derived from miniature wargames and is commonly recognized as the foundation of the role-playing game industry. Each player is assigned a specific character to play who then embarks upon imaginary adventures within a fantasy setting.

Together, characters solve dilemmas, engage in battles, and gather knowledge and treasure. In the process the characters earn experience points to become increasingly powerful over a series of sessions. The game has won multiple awards and has been translated into many languages.

Dungeon Master

MATT SAYS:

"Dungeon Master is a role very much akin to being a leader within a business or in politics. There are two kinds of people who become DMs: those that will do it because someone has to and they have the skills, and those eager to do it because it sounds important.

You can probably guess who does the best job and who ruins the game by making it all about them."

QUICK SUMMARY:

Serves as the game's referee and storyteller while maintaining the settings of the adventures. Also plays the role of the world's non-player inhabitants including monsters.

Gene Roddenberry

MATT SAYS:

"Between Roddenberry and Tolkien, it is hard to say who has had a more significant impact on my dreams, world view, and hopes for the future. I'm certainly not the first person to call him a cultural visionary, and I won't be the last."

QUICK SUMMARY:

A television screenwriter and producer best known for producing the original 1966 *Star Trek* television series. The series ran for only three seasons before it was canceled, leading Roddenberry to work on *Star Trek* feature films instead. In 1987, *Star Trek: The Next Generation* was born, a syndication of the original series. Many others have followed, expanding Roddenberry's universe.

He-Man and the Masters of the Universe

MATT SAYS:

"While this show hasn't held up well in my adult eyes, I have to admit that at age 8 it was squarely in my bullseye. I clearly remember standing atop a mountain of our couch cushions with a cardboard wrapping paper tube held aloft, yelling 'I HAVE THE POWEEEEEEERRRRRR!'"Shirtless, of course."

QUICK SUMMARY:

The principal character of a series of comic books and several animated television series, characterized by his superhuman strength. In most variations he is the alter ego of Prince Adam. *He-Man* and his friends attempt to defend the realm of Eternia and the secrets of Castle Grayskull from the evil forces of Skeletor.

He-Man and the Masters of the Universe is an American animated television series, often referred to simply as *He-Man*. It was one of the most popular animated children's shows of the 1980s.

The Jonas Brothers

MATT SAYS:

"I grew up in a generation that saw the boy band commoditized. After NKOTB, Backstreet Boys, and N'Sync, I didn't have much mental energy or patience left for the Jonas boys."

QUICK SUMMARY:

An American pop rock band founded in 2005. The *Jonas Brothers* gained popularity from their appearances on the *Disney Channel*. The band consists of three brothers from Wyckoff, New Jersey: Paul Kevin Jonas II, Joseph Adam Jonas, and Nicholas Jerry Jonas.

The brothers starred in the *Disney Channel* Original Movie *Camp Rock* and its sequel *Camp Rock 2: The Final Jam*. The group also starred in its own *Disney Channel* series, *JONAS*, which was later re-branded for its second season as *Jonas L.A.*

Jonathan Coltrane

MATT SAYS:

"I am not much of a jazz guy, but in our research I have to say I geeked out on Coltrane's legacy. Did you know he was actually canonized after his death by the African Orthodox Church? That's right, Saint Coltrane."

QUICK SUMMARY:

Also known as Trane, Jonathan Coltrane was an American jazz saxophonist and composer heavily active in the jazz music scene from the 1940s to the 1960s. Trane helped pioneer the use of modes in jazz and was later at the forefront of free jazz.

Coltrane was awarded a special Pulitzer Prize in 2007 citing his "masterful improvisation, supreme musicianship, and iconic centrality to the history of jazz." He was inducted into the North Carolina Music Hall of Fame in 2009. His work influenced many musicians and he remains one of the most significant saxophonists in music history.

Magic the Gathering

MATT SAYS:

"So very addictive. *Magic* was a significant drain on my time, money, and attention for many years. I kicked the habit shortly after college and buried my card collection deep in the basement.

If you are a strategic thinker who likes to build something, test it in live fire game environments, and revise through dozens of iterations, *try at your own risk*. The game design was so successful that it spawned dozens of copycats. One called Hearthstone, by Blizzard, is my newest addiction."

QUICK SUMMARY:

The first trading card game ever produced. It is played by two or more people in various formats, the most common of which uses a deck of 60+ cards. Each game represents a battle between wizards known as "planeswalkers." Players employ spells, artifacts, and creatures depicted on individual *Magic* cards to defeat their opponents.

New cards are released on a regular basis through expansion sets. An organized tournament system played at an international level has evolved to include a worldwide community of players. Collectible card games pull in over $1.5 billion each year.

Pathfinder

MATT SAYS:

"*Pathfinder* diverged from *D&D* around the time I took a years-long break from RPGs. By the time I returned, it was very different from what I remembered from my cousin's basement. I was a little intimidated. This is where the die-hards went when *D&D* simplified its rules and became more inclusive."

QUICK SUMMARY:

A fantasy role-playing game (RPG) created in 2009 that extends and modifies the revised third edition of *Dungeons & Dragons* game rules. The game sets itself apart from other RPGs because of its emphasis on tactical combat and heroic fantasy as well as its capacity for detailed character customization.

Pokémon

MATT SAYS:

"I was a little old for *Pokémon* when it came out, but I watched it anyway for a year or so. It was just enough time to be caught up in the nostalgia-driven hysteria of *Pokémon Go*. I had to catch them all for like four months."

QUICK SUMMARY:

The franchise was created in 1995 and centers around fictional creatures called "Pokémon," which humans, known as *Pokémon* Trainers, catch and train to battle each other for sport.

The franchise started with a pair of video games for the original *Game Boy*, but now includes video games, trading card games, animated television shows and movies, comic books, and toys. *Pokémon* is the second best-selling video game franchise, second only to *Mario*.

Renaissance Festivals

MATT SAYS:

"I was never in the drama program at my high school. I got my spotlight fix by dressing up as a monk with a homespun hooded robe and wandering the Minnesota Renaissance Festival. I kept one hand on my 7-foot-tall walking stick and the other on a roasted turkey leg.

My crew and I made it our goal each year to be mistaken by other visitors as paid employees of the fair. We would heckle passers-by, promote our favorite vendors with loud slogans in bad Olde English accents, and frequently burst out reenacted scenes from *Monty Python and the Holy Grail*. 'Bring out your dead.'"

QUICK SUMMARY:

An outdoor weekend gathering that recreates a historical setting for the amusement of its guests. Open to the public and typically commercial in nature, renaissance festivals are often set during the reign of Queen Elizabeth I of England. Visitors are encouraged to participate and wear costumes.

Many festivals welcome fantasy elements such as wizards and elves. Entertainment is provided in the form of musical and theatrical acts and art and handicrafts are made for sale. Learn more about the Minnesota Renaissance Festival at *renaissancefest.com*

Settlers of Catan

MATT SAYS:

"I have a lot of friends who are deeply into this tabletop juggernaut, enough friends that I know better. This is not a game, it is *a hobby* and a slippery slope toward obsession."

QUICK SUMMARY:

A multi-player board game created in 1995. Players take on the role of settlers, each attempting to build and develop holdings while trading and acquiring resources. You are awarded points as your settlements grow. The first to reach a set number of points, typically 10, is the winner.

This German board game has become very popular worldwide and has been translated into 30 languages.

Starfleet

MATT SAYS:

"I read an article by a futurist recently that suggested many of us could live past the age of 250 years. If that turns out to be true, I may still get to pursue my dream career as a Starfleet captain. I already know I can pull off the uniform."

QUICK SUMMARY:

A fictional quasi-military organization in the *Star Trek* franchise maintained by the United Federation of Planets as the principal means for conducting deep-space exploration, research, defense, peacekeeping, and diplomacy. Starfleet officers comprise the Federation's starship crews, the most famous being the USS Enterprise(s). Learn more at *startrek.com*.

Star Trek

MATT SAYS:

"Fans of *Star Trek* have been immersed in a considerable, mostly friendly, debate over the best Starfleet captain. One can draw their own conclusions based on an array of factors, such as Toughest Captain in a Fight, Best Captain to Have a Beer With, Most Attractive Captain, Best Accent, or more commonly, Whoever Was Captain When I Was Fourteen. At the end of the day real Trekkies (or Trekkers *if you prefer*) love all the captains and commanders. Just know that Picard is the best."

QUICK SUMMARY:

Set on a starship in the 2260s, a crew led by Captain James T. Kirk, First Officer and Science Officer Spock, and Chief Medical Officer Leonard McCoy explore space.

"Space, the final frontier. These are the voyages of the starship Enterprise. Its five-year mission: to explore strange new worlds, to seek out new life and new civilizations, *to boldly go where no man has gone before.*

Star Wars

MATT SAYS:

"The proper order of an adult's first exposure to the Star Wars franchise is as follows: begin with the original trilogy (Episodes 4-6), follow with *Rogue One: A Star Wars Story*, then watch the prequels (Episodes 1-3) with the understanding Lucas Arts was trying too hard to capture a new generation of young fans. Just ignore Jar-Jar and he will go away.

Finally, watch any of the new trilogy that are out at the time you read this (Episodes 7-9). While you are waiting, check out the *Clone Wars* and *Rebels* animated series. If you are a true fan, make time to enjoy the *1978 Star Wars Holiday Special,* which originally aired on CBS. It is deep 70s kitsch, but you get to see the introduction of Boba Fett."

QUICK SUMMARY:

A 1977 epic space opera and the first in the *Star Wars trilogy* created by George Lucas. The plot focuses on the Rebel Alliance's attempt to fight back against the Galactic Empire. Properly referred to as *Star Wars: A New Hope*, episode four sets the stage for the adventures of Luke Skywalker, Jedi Master Obi-Wan Kenobi, Princess Leia, Han Solo, and many other now-legendary characters.

The film surpassed *Jaws* as the highest-grossing film of all time when it was first released. Today, it is often regarded as one of the best films of all time, as well as one of the most important films in the history of motion pictures. It has also led to dozens of additional films, shows, books, games, and comics. Learn more at *starwars.com/films*.

Tatooine

MATT SAYS:

"Sure, it was a hive of scum and villainy, but I'd drink there. Great music, glowing cocktails, and people watching that you won't get at your local pub."

QUICK SUMMARY:

A fictional world from the *Star Wars* series. Tatooine is a harsh desert, a lawless place ruled by Hutt gangsters and filled with many dangers, including sandstorms, bands of savage Tusken Raiders, and carnivorous krayt dragons. The planet is also known for its dangerous Podraces, rampant gambling, and legalized slavery. Anakin and Luke Skywalker grew up here and Obi-Wan Kenobi spent his years hiding on this desert planet.

The Hobbit

MATT SAYS:

"Once you have read this book and really accepted it was written in the 30s, you will begin to see the basic storyline almost everywhere: in movies, books, and comics. Tolkien's unassuming little hobbits set the stage for hundreds of other unlikely heroes who discover their inner strength, from Spiderman to Neville Longbottom. In fact, I would like to that think we all have a little hobbit in us.

After all, as Gandalf said, 'It is the small everyday deeds of ordinary folk that keep the darkness at bay. Small acts of kindness and love. Why Bilbo Baggins? Perhaps because I am afraid, and he gives me courage.'"

A children's fantasy novel written by English author J. R. R. Tolkien in 1937, which many consider to have defined the genre. The story is set in a time "between the Dawn of Færie and the Dominion of Men," and follows the quest of hobbit Bilbo Baggins, mysterious wizard Gandalf the Grey, and a band of dwarves to win back the treasure guarded by the dragon Smaug.

The work has remained in print since its release and has seen many adaptations for stage, screen, radio, and board and video games.

The 501st Legion

MATT SAYS:

"I love these humans. The craftsmanship, the attention to detail, the community service work, it all makes me feel like I should try a lot harder at life. Do yourself a favor and check out their website and social media pages for amazing images and stories."

QUICK SUMMARY:

Also known as Vader's First, this is a volunteer organization with over 10,000 active members worldwide. Created in 1997, the Legion is home to Star Wars fans donning the outfits of villains from the films, such as Imperial Stormtroopers, Sith Lords, Clone Troopers, and bounty hunters. Learn more at *www.501st.com.*

"Tribbles in a Shuttle Bay"

MATT SAYS:

"Tribbles are like a cuddly death trap. I want one. Just one. What is the worst that could happen? I'll take really good care of it. Please?"

QUICK SUMMARY:

Tribbles are a fictional alien species from the *Star Trek* universe depicted as small, furry, soft, gentle, attractive, and slow-moving. They usually produce a soothing purring sound when stroked.

Tribbles also reproduce incredibly fast, consuming exponentially larger and larger amounts of food as they multiply and crawl stealthily from one place to another. Starfleet considers them dangerous organisms and forbids their transportation.

Shuttlebay is a facility on a starship where shuttlecraft are launched, received, stored, and maintained. Therefore, to have these dangerous creatures in the shuttlebay would be inviting an epidemic!

Zombie Apocalypse Survival Kits

MATT SAYS:

"My wife and I often discuss our zombie plan. We haven't gotten around to establishing a living will or purchasing a fire extinguisher, but we have worked through several contingencies for an invasion by the walking undead.

She is a bigger zombie geek than me, so I generally bow to her expertise. However, I refuse to accept her risky suggestion we stick near the urban center of Milwaukee in an outbreak. The access to resources simply does not outweigh, in my mind, the increased risk of all those walkers. Get rural and live, simple as that.

What we do agree on is this: we would last longer together than most of the unprepared yahoos out there. Her crossbow/machete and my hunting rifle/softball bat are the kind of combo you see from the grizzled survivors at the end of the movie."

QUICK SUMMARY:

The zombie apocalypse is the fictional notion of a breakdown of society as a result of a zombie outbreak spreading globally. The concept emerged from apocalyptic fiction and has been portrayed in many zombie-related media since *Night of the Living Dead*.

As zombies attack civilization, victims of zombies may become zombies themselves. Eventually, only isolated pockets of survivors remain, scavenging for food and supplies in a world reduced to a pre-industrial hostile wilderness.

This idea has become so popular that even the Center for Disease Control has published a zombie preparedness guide: *www.cdc.gov/phpr/zombies.*

MEET
THE GEEK

ABOUT THE AUTHOR

Matt Meuleners is an
expert consultant and
speaker with nearly
20 years of experience
developing leaders
at every level across
industry sectors. He is
a Managing Partner at
FOCUS Training, Inc. and
Lead Instructor of the
Accelerate and Elevate
Institutes.

Matt teaches Learning & Development at Marquette University
and leads on several non-profit boards, including the Big
Brothers Big Sisters of Greater Milwaukee and the Association of
Talent Development in Southeastern Wisconsin.

More importantly, Matt is a geek. Since the age of eight, he has
been immersed in worlds of science fiction and fantasy, and
especially the communities that have grow out of them.

As a grown-up geek, Matt plays D&D , wears his *Starfleet* uniform
to work, and obsesses over the best way to introduce his sons to
the *Star Wars* movies. He has spent years researching, observing,
and interviewing geeks of all stripes.

GEEK
REFERENCES

Special Thanks to

- Sam "Swords" Catto-Mott, phone interview, July 18, 2016.

- Conrad Bassett-Bouchard, phone interview, June, 22, 2016.

- Matthew Tunnicliffe, phone interview, June 29, 2016.

- Todd Goldsworthy, phone interview, July 20, 2016.

- Scott Lucey, email interview, August 15, 2016.

- Kimberly Beaton, phone interview, September 26, 2016.

- Charlie Koenen, interview, August 2, 2016.

- Kathryn Capri Dougan, email interview, August 3, 2016.

- Thomas Allingham, email interview, June 23, 2016.

- James Turner, "2014 State of the Herd."

- Alyssa Chang, interview, July 7, 2016.

- Natalie Ragusin, email interview, June 21, 2016.

- Karen Kavett, email interview, July 14, 2017.

- Cody Dennean, phone interview, July 19, 2016.

- Joshua Rusch, phone interview, July 19, 2016.

- Nicholas Mork, phone interview, July 27, 2016.

- John Paul Twardowski, interview, January 11, 2018.

- Lynn Richter, email interview, May 25, 2018.

BIBLIOGRAPHY:

Activision. "Company." Accessed March 23, 2017. https://www.activision.com/company/aboutus.

Adkins, Amy. "Employee Engagement in U.S. Stagnant in 2015." *Gallup*, January, 13, 2016. http://news.gallup.com/poll/188144/employee-engagement-stagnant-2015.aspx.

Anders Ericsson, K., Th. Krampe, Ralf, and Tesch-Romer, Clemens. "The Role of Deliberate Practice in the Acquisition of Expert Performance." *Psychological Review* 100, no. 3 (1993): 363-406.

Baldoni, John. "Employee Engagement Does More than Boost Productivity." *Harvard Business Review*, July 4, 2013. https://hbr.org/2013/07/employee-engagement-does-more.

Barista: The Battle for the Perfect Cup Is On. Directed by Rock Baijnauth. Los Angeles, CA: Premiere Digital Services, 2015.

Bronies: The Extremely Unexpected Adult Fans of My Little Pony. Directed by Laurent Malaquais. Los Angeles, CA: BronyDoc, LLC, 2013.

Duckworth, Angela. *Grit: The Power of Passion and Perseverance.* New York: Scribner, 2016.

Erickson, Robin. "Benchmarking Talent Acquisition: Increasing Spend, Cost Per Hire, and Time to Fill." *Bersin*. Last modified April 23, 2015. http://blog.bersin.com/benchmarking-talent-acquisition-increasing-spend-cost-per-hire-and-time-to-fill/.

Kretkowski, Paul D. "The 15 Percent Solution." *Wired*, January 23, 1998. https://www.wired.com/1998/01/the-15-percent-solution/.

Laurent Malaquais, dir. Bronies: The Extremely Unexpected Adult Fans of My Little Pony. 2012; Studio City: BronyDoc, LLC, 2013. DVD.

NASA. "A Gravity Assist Primer." Basics of Space Flight. Accessed March 19, 2018. https://solarsystem.nasa.gov/basics/primer/.

"Ravenwood Castle in New Plymouth, OH needs a Chief Game Instructor/Assistant Innkeeper!" Press Releases. Last modified June 6, 2014. https://boardgamegeek.com/thread/1183439/ravenwood-castle-hiring-chief-game-instructorassis.

Sinek, Simon. *Start with Why*: How Great Leaders Inspire Everyone to Take Action. London: Portfolio/Penguin, 2013.

Tenenbaum, David. "Josh Medow: Critical Care For the Brain." *W News*. Last modified September 3, 2015. http://news.wisc.edu.josh-medow-critical-care-for-the-brain/.

Turner, James. "2014 State of the Herd Report." 2014 Report. Last modified February 15, 2014. http://www.herdcensus. com/2014%20STATE%20OF%20THE%20HERD%20REPORT.pdf.

University of Wisconsin-Madison. "Forward Motion - Brain Pressure Monitor Implant." Facebook, October 23, 2012. https://www.youtube.com/watch?list=PLoOaFCJQANyx7_ TennkcFKtyJsJziTmbA&v=70nI1l1lH6U.

Vlahos, Kelley Beaucar. "Rise of the Bronies." *The American Conservative*. January 3, 2014. http://www. theamericanconservative.com/articles/rise-of-the-bronies/.

WikiHow. "How to Make Chain Mail," Accessed March 19,2018. https://www.wikihow.com/Make-Chainmail.

Williams Jr., John D. *Word Nerd: Dispatches from the Games, Grammar, and Geek Underground*. New York: Liveright Publishing Corporation, 2016.

Wozniak, Steve. *iWoz: Computer Geek to Cult Icon: How I Invented the Personal Computer, Co-Founded Apple, and Had Fun Doing It*. New York: W.W. Norton & Company, 2006.

GEEK OUT

AT GEEKDEEPBOOK.COM

Read more geek stories, connect to the geekosystem, and learn more about the power of masters, makers, and missionaries!

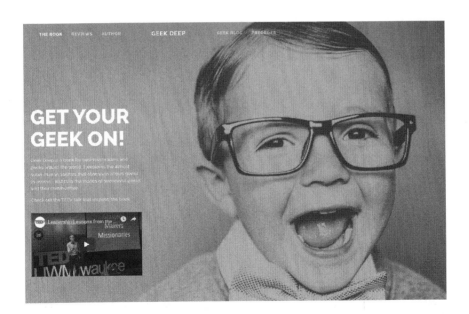

Made in the USA
Columbia, SC
01 November 2019

82361151R00100